D0653135

Mediterranean Cuisine

Mediterranean Cuisine

Contents

Starters, soups and snacks

Acquacotta
vegetable soup with egg

Serves 4

1 onion

3 sticks celery with green leaves

6 tomatoes

½ bunch each of basil and parsley

3 tbsp olive oil

1.5 l vegetable stock

salt

pepper

4 slices stale bread

4 eggs

Preparation time: approx.
15 minutes (plus cooking time)
Per serving approx. 372 kcal/
1564 kJ
15 g P, 23 g F, 26 g CH

1 Peel and chop the onion. Clean, wash, string and dice the celery and chop the leaves. Score the tomatoes with a cross, scald with boiling water, remove the cores, peel, remove the stalks, deseed the flesh and dice. Wash the herbs, shake dry and chop.

2 Heat the oil in a saucepan and fry the onion until transparent. Add the celery and leaves and continue to braise. Add the diced tomatoes and the herbs to the pan and pour on the stock. Season with salt and pepper. Simmer the soup for approx. 15 minutes.

3 Toast the bread, allow to cool then break into pieces. Distribute the bread amongst the 4 soup bowls. Add the eggs to the hot soup individually so that they do not melt away. Allow to steep in the soup for 2 minutes. Then stir with a fork. Pour the soup into the bowls and serve.

Pumpkin soup
with Parmesan

Serves 4

1 carrot
1 onion
½ stick celery
2 tomatoes
400 g pumpkin
200 g potatoes
2 tbsp olive oil
1 l beef stock
salt
pepper
nutmeg
pinch of Cayenne pepper
50 g grated Parmesan

Preparation time: 20 minutes
Per serving approx. 295 kcal/
1235 kJ
22 g P, 14 g F, 19 g CH

1 Peel the carrot and onion, wash the celery and chop all three vegetables finely. Peel, deseed and chop the tomatoes. Peel the pumpkin and potatoes and cut into cubes.

2 Heat the olive oil in a pan and fry the onion until translucent. Add the carrots and celery and fry. Stir in the tomato and potato and fry before pouring over the beef stock. Season with salt and cook the vegetables for approx. 20 minutes until tender.

3 Strain the soup through a sieve and season with pepper, nutmeg and Cayenne pepper. Bring to a boil and stir in the Parmesan. Serve hot.

Minestrone
with pesto

Serves 4

30 g dried porcini

1.5 l vegetable stock

3 aubergines

100 g courgettes

1 Savoy cabbage

50 g pumpkin

4 tomatoes

100 g green beans

3 potatoes

150 g white beans

2 tbsp olive oil

100 g rice

150 g pesto

salt

pepper

Preparation time: 35 minutes
Per serving approx. 410 kcal/
1717 kJ
16 g P, 11 g F, 59 g CH

1 Soak the porcini in water. Bring the vegetable stock to a boil in a pot. Cut the aubergines and courgettes into cubes, slice the cabbage finely, peel and cube the pumpkin and chop the tomatoes into small pieces. Wash the green beans and slice finely. Peel and dice the potatoes.

2 Add the white beans and the rest of the vegetables to the boiling stock. Cut the porcini into small pieces and add to the pot along with the olive oil. Cook the soup for approx. 20 minutes, then add the rice and simmer everything for another 20 minutes. Stir the pesto into the soup before serving and season to taste with salt and pepper.

Lemon bouillon
with Parmesan

Serves 4

400 ml lamb stock
400 ml beef stock
1 tbsp lemon juice
3 egg yolks
70 g freshly grated Parmesan
pepper
1 marjoram stem

Preparation time: approx.
15 minutes
Per serving approx. 130 kcal/
544 kJ
10 g P, 10 g F, 1 g CH

1 Bring the lamb and beef stocks to the boil, allow to bubble for 5 minutes, then put to one side.

2 Mix together the lemon juice and egg yolk. Add 60 g grated Parmesan. Whilst constantly stirring, pour the hot stock on gradually, not allowing it to boil.

3 Season the stock with pepper. Wash the marjoram, shake dry and remove the leaves. Before serving, sprinkle the soup with a few marjoram leaves and the remaining Parmesan.

Bouillabaisse
French fish soup

Serves 4

1 kg mixed ready-to-cook fish
1 onion
4 potatoes
4 tomatoes
½ bulb fennel
4 tbsp olive oil
4 bay leaves
herbes de Provence
salt
pepper
4 sachets saffron
4 garlic cloves
500 ml vegetable stock
500 ml fish stock

Preparation time: 25 minutes (plus cooking and standing time)
Per serving approx. 483 kcal/ 2029 kJ
42 g P, 19 g F, 23 g CH

1 Cut the fish into pieces. Peel and chop the onion. Wash, peel and grate the potatoes. Wash the tomatoes, deseed and cut into dice. Wash the fennel and cut into strips.

2 Heat the olive oil in a pan and braise the onion. Add the potatoes, tomatoes and fennel, and fry. Add the bay leaves and season with the herbs and spices. Peel and crush the garlic and add it to the pan. Leave everything to simmer for 10 minutes, then add the fish and cook for another 3 minutes.

3 Heat both the vegetable and the fish stock, mix everything together, remove from the heat and leave the soup to stand for 10 minutes. Garlic bread makes a great accompaniment.

Zuppa di Fontina
cheese soup

Serves 4

100 g wafer-thin slices of bread

400 g Fontina cheese

1.25 l meat stock

Preparation time: approx. 20 minutes

Per serving approx. 446 kcal/ 1868 kJ

29 g P, 29 g F, 15 g CH

1 Toast the slices of bread and then put 1 slice each into 4 soup bowls – preferably with lids. Slice the cheese very thinly and place 1 slice on top of the bread slice in each bowl.

2 Then layer the bread and cheese slices alternately until the ingredients are all used up.

3 Bring the meat stock to the boil and pour over the bread and cheese mixture. Place the lids on the soup bowls. Allow to steep for about 5 minutes in a warm oven and serve immediately.

Gazpacho
chilled vegetable soup

Serves 4

400 g ripe tomatoes
1 onion
1 garlic clove
½ cucumber
1 red pepper
1 green pepper
2 slices of white bread
4 tbsp olive oil
2 tbsp sherry vinegar
salt
freshly ground black pepper

Preparation time: 20 minutes (plus standing time)
Per serving approx. 170 kcal/ 710 kJ
4 g P, 11 g F, 14 g CH

1 Score crosses into the tomatoes, scald briefly in boiling water, then douse in cold water and skin. Cut the tomatoes into quarters, deseed and remove the cores. Dice the flesh.

2 Peel the onion and garlic. Wash and peel the cucumber and slice in half lengthways, then cut into 6 cm thick pieces. Wash and halve the peppers, cut out the cores, membranes and seeds, then chop the flesh into bite-sized pieces.

3 Remove a section of the onion and chop it into small dice. Do the same with a quarter of the pepper and a little of the cucumber. Place these vegetables in a separate bowl and set to one side.

4 Blend the rest of the vegetables, onion, garlic and white bread together in a food processor until it is a smooth purée. Stir the olive oil and vinegar into the puréed vegetables. Season to taste with salt and pepper.

5 Cover the soup and leave it to stand in the fridge for at least an hour. Pour the gazpacho into bowls and scatter the finely chopped vegetables over the top.

Stracciatella
alla Romana

Serves 4

4 eggs

1 litre strong meat stock

4 tbsp freshly grated Parmesan

salt

pepper

nutmeg

Preparation time: approx.
25 minutes
Per portion approx. 169 kcal/
706 kJ
14 g P, 11 g F, 2 g CH

1 Beat the eggs in a bowl using a balloon whisk, until frothy. Fold in 125 ml cold meat stock and the Parmesan. Season with salt, pepper and a little freshly grated nutmeg.

2 Bring the remaining meat stock to the boil in a saucepan. Briefly remove from the hob and whilst constantly stirring, gradually add the egg mixture.

3 Put the pan back on the hob and simmer again for 5 minutes on a low heat. Stir vigorously with the balloon whisk until small shreds of egg form.

4 Pour into pre-warmed soup dishes and serve immediately. Serve with fresh white bread.

Spanish-style soup
with chicken

Serves 4

1 ready-to-cook chicken
(approx. 1.8 kg)
2 bags soup greens
2 garlic cloves
salt
2 beef tomatoes
2 courgettes
1 Spanish onion
1 tsp dried oregano
150 g spaghetti
1 red pepper
1 green pepper
150 g frozen peas
pepper
paprika

Preparation time: 40 minutes (plus
cooking time)
Per serving approx. 992 kcal/
4153 kJ
66 g P, 61 g F, 40 g CH

1 Cut the chicken in half and place in a pot with the chopped soup greens. Fill the pot with 2 litres of water, add the peeled garlic and bring everything to a boil.

2 Season with salt, half-cover the pot with a lid and simmer over a low heat for approx. 1½ hours.

3 Skin, deseed, core and dice the tomatoes, dice the courgettes and slice the onion into strips.

4 Take the chicken out of the pot, strain the broth through a sieve and then bring it back to a boil. Add the vegetables and the oregano, bring the mixture to a boil, then add the spaghetti and cook according to the packet instructions.

5 Cut the peppers into thin strips. Strip the meat from the chicken and cut into slices. Remove the skin. Add the peppers, peas and meat to the soup and simmer everything for 5 minutes. Season to taste with salt, pepper and paprika.

Bruschetta
with tomatoes

Serves 4

2 garlic cloves

2 beef tomatoes

salt

pepper

½ bunch basil

8 slices white bread or
baguette

6 tbsp olive oil

Preparation time: 25 minutes (plus
grilling time)
Per serving approx. 178 kcal/
749 kJ
3 g P, 10 g F, 20 g CH

1 Pre-heat the grill to 200 °C (Gas Mark 6, fan oven 180 °C). Peel the garlic cloves. Wash and halve the beef tomatoes, remove the cores and seeds, and cut into small dice.

2 Sprinkle the tomato pieces with salt and pepper. Wash the basil, shake dry and tear the leaves from their stalks. Slice the leaves and mix with the tomatoes.

3 Grill the slices of bread on both sides until golden brown. Remove from the grill and rub the sides with the garlic cloves. Drizzle the olive oil over the bread and divide the tomato mixture among the slices.

Spinach flan
with Fontina and Parmesan

For a 1.5 l flan dish

80 g butter

80 g plain flour

250 ml milk

250 ml vegetable stock

salt

pepper

freshly grated nutmeg

1 kg fresh spinach

2 eggs

125 g freshly grated
   Parmesan

125 g diced Fontina cheese

butter and breadcrumbs for
   flan dish

Preparation time: approx.
25 minutes (plus cooking time)
Per portion approx. 637 kcal/
2675 kJ
34 g P, 46 g F, 20 g CH

1 Melt the butter in a pan and make a roux with the flour. Add the milk and the stock; whilst stirring, make a béchamel sauce. Season with salt, pepper and nutmeg.

2 Wash and sort the spinach; put in a pan dripping wet and heat. When the spinach has wilted, take it out, squeeze out the water and chop.

3 Mix the eggs, Parmesan and Fontina with the béchamel sauce and season to taste with salt, pepper and nutmeg.

4 Grease a flan dish with butter and sprinkle with breadcrumbs. Add the spinach.

5 Put the flan dish in the oven, in a drip pan filled with water, and bake the flan for 40 minutes at 200 °C (Gas Mark 6, fan-assisted ovens 180 °C). Then turn it out of the dish and slice. Serve as a starter or a side dish.

Artichokes
in tomato sauce

Serves 4–6

12 small artichokes

juice of 1 lemon

200 g plain flour

50 ml sunflower oil

400 g sieved tomatoes
(passata)

vegetable stock

salt

pepper

1 tsp freshly chopped thyme

1 tbsp freshly chopped basil

Preparation time: approx.
25 minutes (plus frying and
cooking time)
Per serving approx. 417 kcal/
1750 kJ
14 g P, 14 g F, 58 g CH

1 Clean the artichokes. Cut off all but 3 cm of the stalk and peel, remove the hard outer leaves, chop off the leaf tips and cut the artichokes into four pieces.

2 Place the artichokes in a bowl with water and the lemon juice. Put the flour on a plate. Heat the oil in a pan. Remove the artichokes from the lemon water and pat dry thoroughly. Toss in the flour and fry in the hot oil until light brown.

3 Add the tomatoes and fill the pan with stock so that the artichokes are covered. Season with salt and pepper and simmer for a further 20 minutes or so, until the sauce thickens. Season with thyme and basil.

Beef carpaccio

Serves 4

300 g fillet of beef, fat and
  tendons removed

1 stick celery

2 tbsp lemon juice

6 tbsp olive oil

salt

pepper

50 g Parmesan or Grana
  Padano

Preparation time: 20 minutes
(plus freezing and marinating
time)
Per serving approx. 260 kcal/
1092 kJ
19 g P, 19 g F, 2 g CH

1 Leave the fillet of beef in the freezer for approx. 1 hour until it is slightly frozen, then take out and cut into wafer-thin slices.

2 Wash the celery and cut the green parts into small dice. Mix the lemon juice with oil and salt and stir until it forms a smooth sauce.

3 Place the slices of meat on a plate and sprinkle with freshly ground pepper. Drizzle the sauce over the carpaccio.

4 Leave the carpaccio to stand for approx. 30 minutes, covered with foil. Then scatter shavings of cheese over the meat and add the celery cubes.

Vitello tonnato
veal with tuna sauce

Serves 6

600 g veal (from the shank)
1 stick celery
1 carrot
1 onion
3 cloves
1 bay leaf
500 ml white wine
1 tsp salt
140 g canned tuna
3 anchovy fillets in brine
2 egg yolks
3 tbsp pickled capers
juice of 1 lemon
100 ml olive oil
black pepper

Preparation time: 45 minutes
(plus marinating, cooking and
cooling time)
Per serving approx. 380 kcal/
1590 kJ
26 g P, 25 g F, 7 g CH

1 Wash the veal with cold water and pat dry, then place in a pot. Wash the celery, cut off the green parts and cut into 4 pieces of equal size. Wash the carrot, cut away the top and end, peel and cut into 3 cm lengths. Peel the onion and cut into quarters. Poke the cloves through the bay leaf. Add the spices and the vegetables to the meat along with the white wine. Marinate the meat for 24 hours, turning several times.

2 The next day, pour in enough water to cover the meat. Add salt and bring to a boil. Simmer the meat over a low heat, uncovered, for an hour until cooked, then leave to cool in its broth.

3 Drain the tuna. Rinse the anchovies with cold water and chop roughly. Blend the tuna to a smooth purée with the anchovies, egg yolk, 2 tablespoons of the capers and the lemon juice. Stir in a little of the veal stock and the olive oil, little by little, until you have a velvety sauce. Season with salt and pepper.

4 Slice the veal as finely as possible – a kitchen slicer or electric knife would work best – and arrange on a platter. Pour the tuna sauce over the top and keep cold for at least 2 hours. Scatter over the rest of the capers before serving. White bread goes well with vitello tonnato, especially for dipping in the sauce.

Empanadillas
with mushrooms and prawns

Serves 4

1 pack frozen puff pastry
butter
2 chopped onions
2 chopped tomatoes
1 chopped green pepper
250 g mixed mushrooms
1 tbsp oil
salt
pepper
1 hard-boiled egg
100 g ready-to-cook prawns
½ tsp chilli powder
1 egg yolk for coating

Preparation time: 25 minutes
(plus baking time)
Per serving approx. 236 kcal/
992 kJ
12 g P, 16 g F, 12 g CH

1 Leave the puff pastry to thaw. Pre-heat the oven to 200 °C (Gas Mark 6, fan oven 180 °C). Heat the butter and fry the onions. Stir in the tomatoes and the pepper. Wash the mushrooms and chop a little, depending on their size. Heat 1 tablespoon of oil in a pan and fry the mushrooms over a high heat. Season with salt and pepper.

2 Peel the egg and chop into small pieces. Chop the prawns into small pieces. Fry the egg and prawns together. Add the chilli and cook the mixture on a low temperature for 10 minutes, stirring occasionally. Season with salt and pepper and leave to cool.

3 Roll out the puff pastry and cut out a circle with a diameter of 15 cm. Place the filling on one half of the circle. Dampen the edges with a little water, fold over and press closed. Brush with the beaten egg yolk and bake for 15 minutes.

Baked tortilla
on skewers

Serves 4

aluminium foil
oil for the tin
1–2 garlic cloves
4 spring onions
1 red pepper
1 green pepper
oil for frying
3 cooked potatoes
5 eggs
75 g sour cream
150 g freshly grated Spanish
   cheese, e.g. Roncal
2 tbsp chives
salt
pepper
wooden skewers for serving

Preparation time: 25 minutes
(plus baking time)
Per serving approx. 523 kcal/
2195 kJ
23 g P, 42 g F, 15 g CH

1 Line a rectangular baking tin (approx. 18 x 25 cm) with aluminium foil and grease with oil. Pre-heat the oven to 180 °C (Gas Mark 4, fan oven 160 °C).

2 Peel and crush the garlic and wash the spring onions and cut into small pieces. Wash and halve the peppers. Remove the seeds and cores and cut the flesh into small dice.

3 Heat a little oil, fry the spring onions and add the crushed garlic. Stir in the peppers, fry everything for approx. 8 minutes, then leave to cool.

4 Cut the potatoes into small dice and mix with the vegetables. Whisk the eggs and mix them with the sour cream, cheese and chives. Fold in the vegetable mixture and add salt and pepper.

5 Pour everything into the baking tin and shake until flat. Bake for approx. 35 minutes in the pre-heated oven at 180 °C (Gas Mark 4, fan oven 160 °C). The tortilla should be cooked all the way through.

6 Take the dish out of the oven, cut into cubes and serve on wooden skewers.

Pickled olives
with garlic and onions

Serves 4

approx. 250 g large olives
(from a jar)

1 large onion

3 garlic cloves

1 bay leaf

3 tbsp red wine vinegar

3 tbsp olive oil

Preparation time: 15 minutes
(plus cooking and standing time)
Per serving approx. 132 kcal/
554 kJ
1 g P, 12 g F, 3 g CH

1. Drain the olives in a sieve. Peel the onion and chop finely. Wash the unpeeled garlic cloves and press flat with the edge of a knife.

2. Cut around the olives lengthways until you hit the stones.

3. Place the olives in a pan with the onion, garlic, bay leaf and vinegar, and pour in water until just covered. Pour the olive oil on top of the water.

4. Bring the contents of the pan to a boil and then leave to simmer for approx. 4–6 hours. Cook the olives until they are done and the water has almost evaporated.

5. Put everything in a jar, seal it tight and leave to stand for several days.

Pumpkin slices
with tomatoes and ricotta

Serves 4

500 g pumpkin flesh
olive oil
salt
pepper
3 tomatoes
1 garlic clove
100 g ricotta
2 tbsp basil in strips

Preparation time: approx.
30 minutes (plus cooking time)
Per serving approx. 131 kcal/
549 kJ
5 g P, 9 g F, 8 g CH

1 Pre-heat the oven to 180 °C (Gas Mark 4, fan oven 160 °C). Peel the pumpkin, remove the seeds and cut the flesh into slices. Grease a baking sheet, place the sliced pumpkin on it and season with salt and pepper. Bake in the oven until the slices of pumpkin are soft.

2 Score the tomatoes with a cross, scald with boiling water, remove the skins, stalks and seeds, then dice. Peel the garlic and chop finely. Cut the ricotta into slices.

3 Mix the diced tomatoes with the garlic, spices and basil, and lay on top of the sliced pumpkin. Place 1 slice of ricotta on each slice of pumpkin and melt in the oven. Serve immediately.

Stuffed dates
with prosciutto

Serves 4

12 fresh dates
125 g mild goat's cheese
1 orange
pinch of Cayenne pepper
sea salt
12 thin slices of prosciutto
12 sprigs rosemary
2 tbsp oil
3 tbsp lemon juice
red peppercorns

Preparation time: 15 minutes
(plus baking time)
Per serving approx. 400 kcal/
1680 kJ
18 g P, 19 g F, 39 g CH

1 Pre-heat the oven to 180 °C (Gas Mark 4, fan oven 160 °C). Pit the dates and score them lengthways. Cut the cheese into 12 pieces.

2 Wash the orange with hot water, then dry it and strip off a little of the peel with a zester. Stuff the dates with the cheese and orange zest. Sprinkle with a little Cayenne pepper and salt.

3 Wrap each date in a slice of prosciutto and stick a sprig of rosemary through it.

4 Arrange the dates on a baking tray, drizzle over a little oil and bake in the oven for 10 minutes.

5 Drizzle the lemon juice over the hot dates, sprinkle with red pepper and serve warm.

Tuna tramezzini
with capers

Serves 4

140 g canned tuna in brine

2 anchovy fillets in brine

1 tbsp pickled capers

2 tbsp double cream cheese

4 tbsp lemon juice

salt

black pepper

16 slices white sandwich
   bread

Preparation time: 20 minutes
(plus cooking time)
Per serving approx. 691 kcal/
2902 kJ
17 g P, 31 g F, 79 g CH

1 Drain the tuna and flake it roughly with a fork. Drain the anchovies and capers. Rinse the anchovies under cold running water. Chop the capers and anchovies roughly with a large kitchen knife. Put the tuna, anchovies and capers in a bowl, add the cream cheese and lemon juice and stir until the mixture is smooth. Season to taste with salt and pepper.

2 Cut the crusts off the slices of bread. Spread 8 slices with the tuna paste. Place the other slices on top and press down lightly. Slice the tramezzini diagonally and arrange on plates.

Pasta, rice and grains

Spaghetti bolognese
a classic dish

Serves 4

1 onion

1 garlic clove

75 g streaky bacon

1 carrot

½ stick celery

2 tbsp olive oil

400 g minced meat

100 ml red wine

salt

pepper

100 ml milk

1 tsp freshly chopped
   oregano

400 g chopped tinned
   tomatoes

1 tbsp sugar

400 g spaghetti

50 g grated Parmesan

thyme for garnishing

Preparation time: 30 minutes
(plus cooking time)
Per serving approx. 733 kcal/
3069 kJ
41 g P, 28 g F, 76 g CH

1 Peel and chop the onion and garlic. Cut the bacon into cubes. Peel the carrot, wash the celery, and cube both. Heat the oil and fry the bacon. Add the vegetables and then the mince, and fry until the meat is brown, stirring constantly.

2 Pour in the red wine and leave the mixture to simmer until the liquid has boiled off. Season with salt and pepper. Stir in the milk, and boil the sauce down until it is smooth. Stir the oregano, tomatoes and sugar into the sauce and cook everything until tender over a low heat for approx. 30 minutes.

3 In the meantime, cook the spaghetti until *al dente* according to the packet instructions, then drain. Transfer to plates, divide the sauce between the spaghetti, sprinkle over the Parmesan and serve garnished with thyme.

Bucatini
with Gorgonzola and ham

Serves 4

400 g bucatini
150 g Gorgonzola
250 ml cream
salt
pepper
sugar
150 g slices Parma ham
1 bunch parsley

Preparation time: 25 minutes
Per serving approx. 905 kcal/
3789 kJ
35 g P, 46 g F, 87 g CH

1 Cook the bucatini according to the packet instructions. Remove the Gorgonzola rind, cut the cheese into cubes and melt in a wide pan over a low heat.

2 Stir in the cream, season with salt, pepper and sugar, and leave the mixture to boil down for approx. 3–5 minutes, stirring occasionally.

3 Cut the slices of ham in half and warm in the cheese sauce. Wash, dry and finely chop the parsley.

4 Mix the bucatini with the Gorgonzola sauce and serve sprinkled with the parsley.

Spaghetti
with pesto

Serves 4

1 tbsp pine nuts

1½ bunch basil

1 garlic clove

salt

3 tbsp Parmesan

60 ml olive oil

pepper

500 g spaghetti

Preparation time: 30 minutes
Per serving approx. 518 kcal/
2169 kJ
17 g P, 11 g F, 86 g CH

1 Toast the pine nuts in a dry pan. Tear the basil leaves from their stalks, then wash and dry. Peel the garlic and chop roughly together with the pine nuts and basil.

2 Blend the basil, garlic, pine nuts and salt to a paste. Stir in the Parmesan and olive oil, and season with pepper.

3 In the meantime, cook the spaghetti in plenty of salted water according to the packet instructions, until *al dente*. Mix with the pesto and serve.

Ravioli

with mushroom stuffing

Serves 4

400 g flour
5 eggs
salt
40 g butter
400 g mushrooms
1 garlic clove
100 g onions
100 ml white wine
1 bunch flat-leaf parsley
½ bunch thyme
pepper
100 g ricotta
40 g Parmesan
4 tbsp olive oil
300 g tomatoes
2 tbsp chives

Preparation time: 35 minutes
(plus resting and cooking time)
Per serving approx. 714 kcal/
2989 kJ
26 g P, 30 g F, 77 g CH

1 Mix the flour, 4 eggs, 1 teaspoon of salt and 1–2 tablespoons of water together to form a stretchy dough. Wrap in cling film and place in the fridge to cool for 30 minutes. Heat the butter, dice the mushrooms and fry for 3 minutes in the butter. Add the chopped garlic clove and the chopped onions and fry for 2–3 minutes. Deglaze the pan with the wine. Add the bunch of parsley and the chopped leaves of the ½ bunch of thyme, and cook for another 3 minutes. Season with salt and pepper and leave to cool.

2 Separate the remaining egg. Mix the mushroom mixture with the ricotta, 20 g finely grated Parmesan and the egg yolk. Roll the dough out on a floured surface until it is about the thickness of 2 plates (2–3 mm) and cut it into 4 wide strips, each about 10 cm wide. Spoon the filling onto 2 of the strips every 3–4 cm, leaving about 1 cm free around the edges. Whisk the egg white with 2 tablespoons of water, and brush it between the mounds of filling. Place the remaining strips of dough on top of the first two, press down lightly around the filling and cut through the areas in between with a pastry wheel.

3 Cook the ravioli for 6–8 minutes until *al dente*, then fry briefly in olive oil. Skin and dice the tomatoes, add them to the ravioli, fry for 1 minute, and then add salt and pepper. Grate the rest of the Parmesan over the top, and serve sprinkled with the chives.

Ricotta gnocchi
with sausage ragout

Serves 4

500 g ricotta

4 egg yolks

salt

black pepper

1 pinch nutmeg

100 g plain flour

100 g freshly grated
Parmesan

For the sauce:

1 onion

2 garlic cloves

2 sprigs rosemary

1 sprig oregano

1 sprig thyme

2 small sticks celery

1 carrot

3 small pork sausages

2 tbsp olive oil

1 tin peeled tomatoes

125 ml red wine

salt

black pepper

freshly grated Parmesan for
sprinkling

Preparation time: approx.
30 minutes (plus frying time)
Per serving approx. 276 kcal/
1157 kJ
38 g P, 57 g F, 29 g CH

1 Drain the ricotta well and stir with the egg yolk until smooth. Season with salt, pepper and nutmeg. Mix the cheese and egg combination with the flour and stir. Allow the dough to rest for 30 minutes.

2 To make the sauce, peel the onion and garlic, and dice finely. Wash the herbs, shake dry and chop. Wash the celery and peel the carrot. Dice both very finely. Press the sausages from their skins in small pieces.

3 Heat the olive oil in a pan. Sauté the onion, garlic, vegetables and herbs in the oil, and fry the pieces of sausage with the mixture. Mash the tomatoes and put them in the pan with the juice and red wine. Cook for 30 minutes without a lid on a low temperature; season with salt and pepper.

4 In the meantime, bring some salted water to the boil in a large saucepan. Using two damp teaspoons cut out little dumplings from the ricotta mixture and slip them into the boiling water. Half cover the pan with the lid and allow the gnocchi to steep for 10 minutes. Then lift them out of the water using a slotted spoon and place on pre-warmed plates. Pour the sauce on top and serve with Parmesan.

Spaghetti
al pomodoro

Serves 4

400 g spaghetti
salt
1–1.5 kg ripe beef tomatoes
2 shallots
1 small chilli
pepper
6 tbsp olive oil
12 fresh basil leaves
200 g mozzarella

Preparation time: 30 minutes
Per serving approx. 553 kcal/
2315 kJ
25 g P, 16 g F, 76 g CH

1 Cook the spaghetti in salted water until *al dente*, according to the packet instructions. Score the tops of the tomatoes with crosses and remove the stalks, cover with boiling water, then take out, skin, deseed and cut the flesh into dice.

2 Peel and chop the shallots. Deseed the chilli and cut into thin strips. Mix the shallots and chilli together, season with salt and pepper, and add the olive oil. Wash and dry the basil leaves and chop. Add the shallot mixture and basil to the tomatoes.

3 Cut the mozzarella into 2 cm cubes. Drain the spaghetti and leave to dry. Place in a cooking pot and toss with the tomatoes and cubes of mozzarella. Heat gently, turning, for 2–3 minutes, until the mozzarella is beginning to melt.

Pasta, rice and grains

Risotto
with Gorgonzola and artichokes

Serves 4

60 g rocket

2 spring onions

2 tbsp butter

1 pinch sugar

500 g risotto rice

8 artichoke hearts (from a
    jar)

1 l vegetable stock

1 lemon

100 g Gorgonzola

salt

pepper

oregano

basil leaves

Preparation time: approx.
20 minutes (plus cooking time)
Per serving approx. 739 kcal/
3032 kJ
24 g P, 35 g F, 71 g CH

1 Wash the rocket, shake dry and chop finely. Wash
the spring onions and cut into fine rings. Heat
1 tbsp butter and brown the spring onions in it. If
necessary, add a pinch of sugar. Add the rice.

2 Drain the artichoke hearts and cut into quarters. Add 250 ml vegetable stock and the quartered artichokes to the rice. Peel the lemon, cut the
flesh into pieces and add to the rice. Simmer the rice
uncovered, stirring frequently, until the liquid is
absorbed.

3 Add a further 250 ml stock and allow to reduce.
Gradually add the remaining stock and cook on
a medium heat for about 20 minutes, covered, stirring frequently. Add a little water if required.

4 Dice the Gorgonzola and mix into the rice with
the remaining butter and the rocket. Finally,
season with salt, pepper, oregano and basil, and
serve.

Pasta

with sardines

Serves 4

8 sardine fillets
1 bulb fennel
2 garlic cloves
½ red chilli
4 tbsp olive oil
350 g linguine
salt
zest of 1 untreated lemon
1 tbsp lemon juice
2 tbsp toasted pine nuts
3 tbsp freshly chopped
    parsley
pepper

Preparation time: 30 minutes
Per serving approx. 458 kcal/
1917 kJ
23 g P, 12 g F, 62 g CH

1 Wash, dry and roughly chop the sardine fillets. Wash the fennel bulb and slice into thin strips. Peel the garlic and cut into thin slices. Wash, dry and finely dice the chilli.

2 Heat 2 tablespoons of the olive oil, add the garlic and chilli and fry, then add the fennel, frying for another 5 minutes and then mixing in the sardines. Cook for another 4 minutes.

3 Cook the pasta in plenty of salted water according to the packet instructions until *al dente*, then drain thoroughly. Mix the lemon zest and juice, pine nuts, parsley, salt and pepper into the sardines. Add to the pasta along with the rest of the oil and mix everything together.

Pappardelle
with hare ragout

Serves 4

400 g ready-to-cook hare
  meat
50 g pancetta
1 onion
1 stick celery
1 carrot
1 beef tomato
2 tbsp olive oil
salt
pepper
½ tsp dried thyme
100 ml dry white wine
125 ml beef stock
400 g pappardelle

Preparation time: 30 minutes
(plus braising time)
Per serving approx. 615 kcal/
2575 kJ
21 g P, 23 g F, 76 g CH

1 Chop the meat into small pieces and the pancetta into little cubes. Peel and chop the onion. Wash, peel and slice the celery and carrot.

2 Score crosses into the beef tomato, cover with boiling water, then skin and chop the flesh.

3 Heat the oil in a pan and fry the cubes of pancetta. Add the hare meat and fry well on all sides. Add the celery, carrot and tomato, and season with salt, pepper and thyme. Add the wine and stock, cover the pot, and simmer the ragout at a low temperature for approx. 1 hour and 20 minutes.

4 While the ragout is cooking, boil the pappardelle in plenty of salted water until *al dente*, then drain thoroughly. Mix the pasta into the hare ragout and serve.

Pasta

with aubergines

Serves 4

3 aubergines
5–6 tbsp oil
1 garlic clove
1 shallot
2 tbsp lemon juice
4 tbsp olive oil
150 g yoghurt
salt
pepper
400 g tagliatelle
100 g firm ricotta
½ bunch chives

Preparation time: 45 minutes
Per serving approx. 443 kcal/
1855 kJ
18 g P, 8 g F, 74 g CH

1 Pre-heat the oven to 225 °C (Gas Mark 7, fan oven 200 °C). Wash and dry the aubergines. Brush two of the aubergines with half of the oil, and bake for approx. 30 minutes on the middle shelf of the oven until the skin is black. Scrape the aubergine flesh from the skin.

2 Peel the garlic clove and the shallot and blend to a fine purée with the aubergine, lemon juice and 4 tablespoons of olive oil. Stir in the yoghurt and season to taste with salt and pepper.

3 Cook the tagliatelle. Crumble the ricotta. Slice the third aubergine.

4 Heat the rest of the olive oil and brown the aubergine slices lightly on both sides.

5 Wash the chives, dry and cut into lengths. Drain the pasta, refresh in cold water and leave to dry.

6 Mix together the tagliatelle, aubergine slices and cheese. Serve with the sauce and sprinkle over the chives.

Pasta, rice and grains   69

Polenta slices
with beef

Serves 4

200 g polenta

salt

1 onion

2 courgettes

2 tbsp olive oil

300 g minced beef

30 g cubed ham

black pepper

4 tbsp tomato purée

40 g butter

20 g freshly grated
Parmesan

Preparation time: 20 minutes
(plus cooking time)
Per serving approx. 500 kcal/
2090 kJ
24 g P, 27 g F, 41 g CH

1 Gradually add the polenta to 1 litre of boiling salted water, stirring constantly with a wooden spoon. Keep the water temperature under the boiling point to prevent lumps from forming. Once all the polenta has been added, lower the temperature and leave to simmer for approx. 30 minutes, stirring briskly. If the mixture becomes too firm while stirring, add boiling water by the tablespoonful; if it is too runny, stir in some more polenta.

2 Turn the finished polenta out onto a large wooden board or a towel sprinkled with semolina, smooth down until it is 5 cm thick and leave to cool.

3 Chop the onion finely. Wash the courgettes and cut into ½ cm thick slices. Heat the oil in a pan and fry the onion until translucent. Add the minced beef and ham cubes and fry until brown and crumbly. Add salt and pepper and stir in the tomato purée and 4 tablespoons of water. Add the courgette slices and simmer everything for approx. 5 minutes. Pre-heat the oven to 150 °C (Gas Mark 2, fan oven 130 °C).

4 Grease a large, shallow ovenproof dish with the melted butter. Cut the firm polenta into 1 cm thick slices. Lay the slices in the dish. Drizzle over the rest of the butter, sprinkle over a few table-spoons of Parmesan and cover with the meat sauce. Bake for approx. 30 minutes on the middle shelf of the oven. Sprinkle once more with Parmesan before serving.

Risotto milanese
with saffron

Serves 4

1 onion
50 g butter
50 ml dry white wine
400 g risotto rice (e.g. Arborio)
1 l vegetable stock
½ tsp saffron threads
50 g freshly grated Parmesan

Preparation time: 15 minutes (plus cooking time)
Per serving approx. 548 kcal/ 2300 kJ
12 g P, 19 g F, 80 g CH

1 Peel and finely chop the onion. Melt 2 tablespoons of butter in a large pot and fry the onion. Add the wine to the onion and cook over a medium heat until the liquid has almost completely boiled down.

2 Add the rice to the pot and fry, stirring, for approx. 1 minute, until it is coated with the butter. Add the stock little by little, and leave to boil down. Only add more stock once what is in the pot has been absorbed by the rice.

3 The rice will be half-cooked after approx. 10 minutes. Stir the saffron threads into the remaining stock and add to the rice.

4 Simmer for another 15 minutes until the rice is creamy yet still firm to the bite.

5 Stir the rest of the butter and the cheese into the rice, cover, and leave the risotto to stand for a few minutes. Ladle onto plates and serve with Parmesan.

Risotto

with porcini

Serves 4

250 g fresh (or 50 g dried) porcini

1 onion

3 tbsp butter

400 g risotto rice

1 l hot vegetable stock

50 ml white wine

salt

pepper

50 g Parmesan

2 tbsp freshly chopped parsley

Preparation time: 30 minutes
Per serving approx. 498 kcal/
2092 kJ
14 g P, 12 g F, 80 g CH

1 Clean the fresh porcini and cut into small pieces. If using dried porcini, soak in 200 ml water. Peel and chop the onion. Heat 2 tablespoons of butter in a pan and sauté the onion and porcini. Add the risotto rice and cook a little longer until the rice looks slightly glassy.

2 Gradually add the vegetable stock and white wine (or 750 ml stock, the wine and the water used for soaking the porcini) until the rice has completely absorbed all the liquid and is creamy. Season with salt and pepper. Grate the Parmesan and stir it into the risotto with the rest of the butter and parsley, then serve.

Classic lasagne
typically Italian

Serves 4

100 g streaky bacon
1 tbsp olive oil
1 onion
2 garlic cloves
350 g mixed mince meat
salt
pepper
paprika
150 ml red wine
500 g peeled plum tomatoes
2 tbsp butter
2 tbsp flour
500 ml milk
nutmeg
500 g lasagne sheets (no
   precooking required)
100 g freshly grated
   Parmesan
butter for greasing the
   baking dish

Preparation time: 30 minutes
(plus baking time)
Per serving approx. 1125
kcal/4710 kJ
45 g P, 64 g F, 91 g CH

1 Cut the bacon into cubes. Heat the oil and fry the bacon cubes. Chop the onion and garlic cloves finely, add to the bacon and fry. Add the minced meat and cook until crumbly, stirring constantly. Season with salt, pepper and paprika, and pour in the red wine. Add the peeled tomatoes with their juice and simmer everything for approx. 10–15 minutes.

2 Make a roux out of the melted butter and the flour, adding the milk. Bring to a boil, stirring, and add salt, pepper and nutmeg. Pour a little of the béchamel sauce into a greased baking dish. Then alternate layers of lasagne sheets, meat sauce and béchamel sauce until the dish is full.

3 Scatter over the grated cheese, cover, and bake in the oven at 180 °C (Gas Mark 4, fan oven 160 °C) for 20 minutes, then uncover and cook for another 10 minutes. Serve with salad.

Cannelloni
with tomatoes and mozzarella

Serves 4

150 g flour

150 g durum wheat semolina

salt

1.5 kg tomatoes

2 garlic cloves

2 tbsp olive oil

pepper

1 bunch basil

50 g preserved anchovies

2 tbsp preserved capers

300 g mozzarella

100 g freshly grated
  Parmesan

flour for the work surface

fat for greasing dish

Preparation time: approx.
50 minutes (plus cooking and
baking time)
Per serving approx. 802 kcal/
3370 kJ
38 g P, 36 g F, 79 g CH

1 Prepare a pasta dough from the flour, semolina, 1 tsp of salt and 150 ml of lukewarm water, and allow to rest.

2 Score the tomatoes with a cross, scald with boiling water, peel, remove the stalks and dice. Peel the garlic and chop. Heat the oil in a frying pan and sauté the tomatoes with the garlic. Cook for about 30 minutes on a low heat until a thickish sauce forms. Season with salt and pepper. Remove 2 ladles of sauce and put to one side.

3 Wash the basil, shake dry and chop. Drain the anchovies and capers and chop. Dice the mozzarella. Mix everything into the tomato sauce and allow to cool.

4 Pre-heat the oven to 200 °C (Gas Mark 6, fan oven 180 °C). Knead the pasta dough well and roll out thinly onto a floured work surface. Cut into squares of 10 x 10 cm and cook in boiling salted water for about 30 seconds. Drain, refresh in cold water and allow to drip.

5 Grease an oven-proof dish. Lay out the pieces of dough, fill with the mixture, roll up and place in the dish. Pour the reserved tomato sauce over the cannelloni and sprinkle the grated cheese on top. Bake in the oven for about 30 minutes until golden.

Spanish paella
a classic dish

Serves 4

200 g deep-frozen squid rings

1 onion

2 garlic cloves

2 small red chillies

1 red pepper

1 green pepper

4 chicken legs

salt

black pepper

pinch of paprika

200 g chorizo (or spicy sausages)

4 tbsp olive oil

250 g parboiled rice

100 ml white wine

1 small packet of saffron (0.2 g)

approx. 500 ml chicken stock

1 untreated lemon

Preparation time: 30 minutes (plus thawing and cooking time)
Per serving approx. 850 kcal/ 3550 kJ
51 g P, 43 g F, 59 g CH

1 Leave the squid rings to thaw. Peel and finely chop the onion and garlic cloves. Wash the chillies and peppers and pat dry, then cut in half lengthways. Finely chop the chillies and cut the peppers into 1 cm pieces.

2 Rinse the chicken legs in cold water, pat dry and rub with salt, pepper and paprika. Skin the sausages and cut into slices.

3 Heat a little oil in a large pan with steep sides. Add the chicken legs and fry over a high heat, approx. 3 minutes on each side, then remove from the pan. Add the rest of the oil to the chicken fat, then add the chopped onion, garlic, chilli and pepper and fry, stirring constantly. Pour in the rice and mix until it looks glassy.

4 Deglaze the vegetable and rice mixture with the white wine. Stir in the saffron. Add salt and pepper, pour in approx. 500 ml of chicken stock and bring to a boil, before adding the chicken legs. Cover the pan and cook for approx. 15 minutes.

5 Top up with stock if necessary to prevent the rice from catching. Add the thawed squid rings and chorizo slices to the paella and cook everything for another 15 minutes. Season everything once again with salt, pepper and paprika. Wash the lemon, cut into eight wedges and serve with the paella.

Red meat and poultry

Fillet of beef
with red wine and herbs

Serves 4

500 g potatoes

500 g courgettes

500 g tomatoes

500 g chanterelles

1 onion

1 garlic clove

4 tbsp olive oil

1.5 kg fillet of beef

salt

pepper

150 ml red wine

50 ml port

3 sprigs thyme

3 sprigs rosemary

3 sprigs sage

4 bay leaves

200 g crème fraîche

Preparation time: 30 minutes
(plus braising time)
Per serving approx. 857 kcal/
3588 kJ
89 g P, 37 g F, 31 g CH

1 Peel the potatoes. Slice the courgettes and potatoes. Skin and slice the tomatoes. Cut the chanterelles into small pieces. Peel and roughly chop the onion and the garlic clove.

2 Heat the oil in a casserole dish and brown the meat well on all sides. Season with salt and pepper. Add the vegetables to the meat, and pour over the red wine and port. Tie the herbs together and place on top of the meat. Cover the dish, and braise in the oven at 200 °C (Gas Mark 6, fan oven 180 °C) for approx. 45 minutes. Once the cooking time is up, take the meat and herbs out and keep the meat warm.

3 Stir the crème fraîche into the roasting juices and season to taste. Serve the sauce with the meat.

Lamb

with tomatoes and garlic

Serves 4

2 garlic cloves
1 sprig rosemary
1 kg lamb
2 tbsp flour
60 ml olive oil
175 ml white wine
salt
pepper
400 g tomatoes
120 ml lamb stock

Preparation time: 25 minutes
(plus braising time)
Per serving approx. 583 kcal/
2441 kJ
75 g P, 25 g F, 6 g CH

1 Peel and chop the garlic cloves. Tear the rosemary leaves from their stems and chop. Wash the lamb, pat dry and cut into cubes. Coat with flour.

2 Heat the oil in a casserole dish and sauté the garlic and rosemary. Add the cubes of lamb and brown thoroughly on all sides, then remove and keep warm. Deglaze with the wine, bring the mixture to a boil and then add the meat once again. Season with salt and pepper.

3 Skin, deseed and dice the tomatoes, and add to the dish along with the lamb stock. Cover the dish and braise for approx. 1 hour 30 minutes in the oven at 180 °C (Gas Mark 4, fan oven 160 °C). Serve with fresh French bread.

Meatballs
with dates and almonds

Serves 4

150 g cooked rice
500 g minced pork
1 egg
20 g toasted almond flakes
salt
pepper
125 g dates
½ lemon
1 tbsp mustard
4 tbsp breadcrumbs
olive oil for frying
4 onions
100 ml white wine
100 ml strong meat stock
2 bay leaves

Preparation time: 25 minutes
(plus cooking time)
Per serving approx. 655 kcal/
2751 kJ
29 g P, 31 g F, 60 g CH

1 Mix the rice with the minced pork, egg and almond flakes, and add salt and pepper. Pit the dates, cut into small pieces and place in a bowl with the meat mixture. Wash and dry the lemon half, grate the zest and add to the other ingredients along with the mustard.

2 Working with damp hands, form small meatballs. Roll the meatballs in the breadcrumbs and fry in the oil. Peel and finely chop the onions. Fry until translucent in a little oil, then pour in the wine and stock. Add the bay leaves. Bring everything to a boil and leave to simmer for approx. 10 minutes.

3 Place the meatballs in the broth and leave to stand for 15 minutes. Leave the meatballs to cool in the broth, then serve with bread.

Roast rabbit
with anchovies

Serves 4

1.5 kg ready-to-cook
   boneless rabbit

4 slices Parma ham

25 anchovy fillets from a jar

pepper

100 g freshly grated
   Parmesan

salt

150 g smoked bacon

2 tbsp olive oil

12 shallots

500 ml dry white wine

5 tomatoes

Preparation time: 30 minutes
(plus braising time)
Per serving approx. 775 kcal/
3245 kJ
95 g P, 41 g F, 4 g CH

1 Spread out the meat on a worktop and place the Parma ham on top. Rinse the anchovy fillets, pat dry, chop 20 of the anchovies and distribute them on the rabbit, then sprinkle over pepper and Parmesan.

2 Roll up the rabbit and tie securely with cooking twine. Rub the outside with salt and pepper. Remove the rind from the bacon and cut into cubes. Heat the oil in a pot and brown the meat thoroughly on all sides, then remove from the pot and set to one side. Fry the bacon and the peeled whole shallots in the roasting fat.

3 Return the meat to the pot, pour in the wine and 100 ml water, cover, and braise in the oven at 160 °C (Gas Mark 3, fan oven 140 °C) for approx. 30 minutes, turning once.

4 Skin, deseed and dice the tomatoes, and add to the rabbit along with the rest of the anchovies once the meat has cooked for 30 minutes. Braise everything for another 20 minutes. Season the sauce with salt and pepper, and serve the meat cut into slices.

Chicken

with oranges and olives

Serves 4

1 ready-to-cook chicken
   (approx. 1.2 kg)

salt

black pepper

3 oranges

½ bunch of rosemary

2 fresh bay leaves

2 onions

1 red chilli pepper

4 tbsp olive oil

100 ml dry Marsala or white
   wine

1 tbsp black olives, stoned

2 tbsp orange marmalade

Preparation time: approx.
35 minutes (plus cooking time)
Per serving approx. 553 kcal/
2310 kJ
52 g P, 19 g F, 38 g CH

1 Divide the chicken into 8 pieces. Rub in salt and pepper. Juice the oranges, wash the rosemary and bay, and dry. Peel and halve the onions and cut into fine strips. Deseed and wash the chilli pepper and slice thinly.

2 Heat the olive oil in a casserole dish. In two portions, sear the chicken pieces well on all sides and remove again. Fry the onions in the oil, add the herbs and deglaze with the orange juice and Marsala. Add the salt, chilli pepper, olives and marmalade.

3 Place the chicken pieces back in the pot and cover. Braise on a low temperature for 40 minutes.

Roast chicken
with fennel

Serves 4

1 ready-to-cook roasting
  chicken (approx. 1.5 kg)

salt

1 onion

120 ml olive oil

2 fennel bulbs

1 garlic clove

pinch of ground nutmeg

pepper

4 thin slices pancetta

120 ml dry white wine

Preparation time: 30 minutes
(plus roasting time)
Per serving approx. 845 kcal/
3538 kJ
66 g P, 61 g F, 4 g CH

1 Rub the inside of the chicken with salt, and stuff it with the quartered onion. Rub the outside with 45 ml of olive oil and place in a large casserole dish, breast side up. Mix the chopped green parts of the fennel with the peeled and chopped garlic clove, nutmeg, salt and pepper, and rub into the chicken. Lay the slices of pancetta over the chicken breast, drizzle with 30 ml of olive oil and roast in the oven at 180 °C (Gas Mark 3, fan oven 160 °C) for approx. 30 minutes.

2 Cook the fennel bulbs in boiling water until *al dente*, and cut into quarters. Turn the chicken, place the fennel around it and drizzle over the rest of the olive oil. Pour over 60 ml of the wine and roast everything for another 30 minutes. Finally, turn the chicken again, pour over the rest of the wine and roast for another 15 minutes until the meat is cooked through.

Florentine steak
grilled to perfection

Serves 4

4 beef steaks, with bone
 (approx. 400 g each)

salt

pepper

Preparation time: 15 minutes
Per serving approx. 295 kcal/
1235 kJ
44 g P, 13 g F, 1 g CH

1 Wash the steaks and pat dry. Grill for approx.
5 minutes on an open grill or using the oven grill
until they have a good crust. Turn the steaks and grill
the other side until crispy. The inside should still be
rare.

2 Season the meat with salt and pepper. Serve hot
with fresh bread and a mixed green salad.

Escalopes
in Marsala sauce

Serves 4

4 pork escalopes

salt

pepper

4 tbsp flour

3 tbsp clarified butter

75 ml Marsala

50 ml beef stock

Preparation time: 10 minutes
(plus frying time)
Per serving approx. 572 kcal/
2404 kJ
41 g P, 33 g F, 28 g CH

1 Beat the escalopes flat. Rub them with salt and pepper and coat with the flour.

2 Heat the clarified butter in a pan and fry the escalopes for 4 minutes on each side, then remove from the pan and keep warm.

3 Deglaze the meat juice with the Marsala and stock, and boil the mixture down until it is a third of its original volume. Arrange the escalopes on plates and serve with the Marsala sauce.

Sicilian

rolled pot-roast

Serves 4

20 g flat parsley

2 eggs

65 ml milk

50 g freshly grated
Parmesan

salt

pepper

375 g beef from the cross-rib

60 g finely sliced ham

65 g olive oil

1 onion

2 tbsp plain flour

250 ml dry red wine

400 ml meat stock

Preparation time: approx.
30 minutes (plus cooking time)
Per serving approx. 534 kcal/
2235 kJ
32 g P, 36 g F, 9 g CH

1 Wash the parsley, shake dry and chop finely. Mix the parsley together with the eggs, milk, Parmesan, salt and pepper. Fry 2 pancakes with the batter.

2 Wash the beef, pat dry and spread out flat. Place the pancakes on top and then cover with the ham, leaving a narrow edge free. Roll up the meat and tie with kitchen twine.

3 Heat up the olive oil in a casserole dish. Sear the meat sharply, then turn down the heat and brown the meat on all sides. Peel the onion and slice. Add to the dish and brown with the meat. Dust with flour and stir everything well.

4 Deglaze with the wine. Pour on the stock, bring to the boil, then reduce the temperature. Braise for an hour, covered, until the meat is cooked and tender. Remove the pot-roast from the pan and cut into pieces. Pour the sauce on the top. Serve with gnocchi.

Ossobuco
veal shanks in tomato and wine sauce

Serves 4

4 veal cutlets, bone in
2 tbsp flour
2 tbsp olive oil
2 onions
1 garlic clove
1 carrot
½ stick celery
200 g tomato passata
200 ml dry red wine
approx. 500 ml beef stock
½ bay leaf
4 tbsp freshly chopped herbs
salt
pepper

Preparation time: 20 minutes
(plus cooking time)
Per serving approx. 263 kcal/
1103 kJ
33 g P, 9 g F, 7 g CH

1 Coat the cutlets in flour and brown thoroughly in hot olive oil in a casserole dish, then remove from the dish.

2 Peel and finely chop the onions and garlic. Wash the carrot and celery, and cut into small pieces. Put the vegetables in a pan with the onions and garlic, and sauté for 3 minutes. Add the tomatoes and pour in the wine. Bring to a boil.

3 Lay the cutlets in the sauce and pour over the stock until everything is completely covered.

4 Add the bay leaf and half of the herbs. Cover the casserole dish with a lid and braise the meat for approx. an hour. After 30 minutes, turn the meat and season.

5 After an hour, remove the bay leaf and stir in the rest of the herbs. If the sauce is too thick, dilute it with a little wine, stock or water. Serve the ossobuco in its sauce.

Saltimbocca
alla Romana

Serves 4

8 thin veal escalopes
   (500 g in total)

1 tbsp flour

salt

black pepper

8 sage leaves

8 slices wafer-thin Parma
   ham

2 tbsp olive oil

2 tbsp butter

125 ml white wine

Preparation time: 15 minutes
(plus cooking time)
Per serving approx. 260 kcal/
1090 kJ
27 g P, 13 g F, 2 g CH

1 Beat the escalopes flat between 2 layers of cling film using a meat mallet or rolling pin. Mix the flour with salt and pepper, and lightly coat the escalopes.

2 Wash the sage leaves and pat dry with kitchen towel. Place a sage leaf and a slice of ham on each escalope. Secure both to the escalope with a wooden skewer or toothpick.

3 Heat the oil and butter in a pan and fry the escalopes for 2 to 3 minutes on each side. Cover with aluminium foil and keep warm in the oven at 50 °C. Deglaze the pan with the wine and bring to a rolling boil. Season with salt and pepper.

4 Serve the saltimbocca on pre-warmed plates. Pasta drizzled with the sauce makes a great accompaniment, along with a colourful leafy salad.

Chicken

Tuscan-style

Serves 4

1 ready-to-cook chicken
(approx. 1.5 kg)

1 onion

2 red peppers

1 garlic clove

2 tbsp olive oil

300 g tinned chopped
tomatoes

150 ml white wine

1 sprig oregano, leaves
removed

salt

pepper

400 g cooked cannellini
beans

1 stale bread roll

Preparation time: approx.
30 minutes (plus cooking and
grilling time)
Per serving approx. 870 kcal/
3654 kJ
85 g P, 43 g F, 28 g CH

1 Wash the chicken, pat dry and cut into 8 pieces. Peel the onion and cut into thin rings. Wash and deseed the peppers and cut into rings. Peel the garlic clove and chop.

2 Heat the oil in a pan and sear the chicken pieces well on all sides. Remove from the pan. Add the onion and pepper rings to the pan and braise until soft. Stir in the garlic. Put the chicken pieces back in the pan. Add the tomatoes, pour on the wine and sprinkle with oregano. Season with salt and pepper. Bring to the boil and simmer uncovered for about 30 minutes until the meat is soft. Fold in the cooked beans and simmer for a further 5 minutes, whilst stirring.

3 In the meantime, pre-heat the grill to the highest temperature. Grate the bread roll. Sprinkle over the pan and put the whole dish under the grill until golden brown. Serve immediately.

Chicken

in lemon and saffron sauce

Serves 4

4 chicken legs

salt

pepper

2 tbsp oil

1 Spanish onion

2 untreated lemons

a few saffron threads

250 ml vegetable stock

½ bunch chopped lemon balm

Preparation time: 15 minutes
(plus frying and cooking time)
Per serving approx. 310 kcal/
1302 kJ
28 g P, 19 g F, 6 g CH

1 Rub the chicken legs with salt and pepper, and fry in the hot oil until they are brown all over. Remove from the pan.

2 Peel the onion, cut into rings, and fry until translucent in the cooking fat. Return the chicken legs to the pan.

3 Wash the lemons in hot water and dry. Squeeze one of the lemons and add the juice to the meat along with the saffron and stock. Cut the second lemon into quarters and add to the pan.

4 Cover the pan and leave everything to braise for approx. 45 minutes. Serve with the chopped lemon balm. Rice makes a good accompaniment for this dish.

Pork loin
with chorizo

Serves 4

600 g pork tenderloin

6 garlic cloves

1 sprig oregano

1 bay leaf

salt

pepper

2 small chorizo sausages
   (approx. 200 g)

1 tsp paprika

50 g pork dripping

Preparation time: 15 minutes
(plus cooking and frying time)
Per serving approx. 595 kcal/
2499 kJ
53 g P, 42 g F, 3 g CH

1 Cut the pork tenderloin into bite-sized pieces. Peel and roughly chop the garlic.

2 Wash the oregano, shake dry and tear the leaves from their stalks. Chop finely.

3 Place the cubes of pork in a stew pot. Add the garlic, oregano, bay leaf and a little salt and pepper. Pour in approx. 175 ml water, then cover and leave to simmer for 10–15 minutes.

4 Cut the chorizo into thin slices and add to the meat. Mix in the paprika and the pork dripping and simmer everything a little longer, uncovered, until the meat is tender and the water has boiled off.

5 Finally, fry the meat thoroughly in the dripping and serve immediately.

Roast lamb
with rosemary

Serves 4

2 garlic cloves

750 g rolled lamb for
   roasting

salt

pepper

2 rosemary sprigs

3 tbsp olive oil

2 tbsp mustard

100 ml white wine

Preparation time: approx.
15 minutes (plus cooking and
resting time)
Per serving approx. 535 kcal/
2247 kJ
35 g P, 42 g F, 2 g CH

1 Peel the garlic cloves and cut into thin batons. Pre-heat the oven to 240 °C (Gas Mark 9, fan oven 220 °C). Wash and pat dry the lamb and rub in salt and pepper. Remove the needles from 1 sprig of rosemary. Stud the lamb with garlic batons and rosemary needles. Brush the meat with the oil.

2 Place the meat in a roasting dish and sear for 15 minutes in the oven. Turn once. Then place the second sprig of rosemary with the meat, brush the meat with the mustard and roast for 20–30 minutes at 200 °C (Gas Mark 6, fan oven 180 °C). Once cooked, remove the meat from the roasting dish, switch off the oven, wrap the meat in aluminium foil and allow to rest for 10 minutes in the oven.

3 Pour the meat juices through a sieve, bring to the boil with the wine and allow to reduce a little. Cut the roast lamb into slices and serve with the gravy.

Veal escalope
with brandy and cream sauce

Serves 4

40 g butter

2 tbsp olive oil

600 g veal escalope

salt

pepper

2 tbsp plain flour

1 unwaxed lemon

2 cl brandy

120 ml meat stock

125 ml cream

Preparation time: approx.
25 minutes
Per serving approx. 428 kcal/
1792 kJ
26 g P, 30 g F, 8 g CH

1 Heat the butter and oil in a frying pan. Wash the meat and pat it dry. Toss the salted and peppered escalopes briefly in flour and sear sharply on both sides in the hot fat.

2 Grate the lemon peel and squeeze out the lemon juice. Deglaze the escalope with brandy. Pour the juice of half the lemon over it and allow to reduce.

3 In the meantime, mix the grated lemon peel with the meat stock and cream.

4 Add the mixture to the meat juices and allow to thicken. Pour the gravy over the escalope and serve.

Spicy pork kebabs
African-style

Serves 4

150 ml olive oil
1 tsp chopped thyme
2 tbsp chopped parsley
1 tsp chilli powder
2 tsp ground cumin
1 tsp mild paprika
pepper
700 g pork
12–16 wooden skewers

Preparation time: 30 minutes
(plus marinating and cooking
time)
Per serving approx. 633 kcal/
2657 kJ
37 g P, 54 g F, 3 g CH

1 Put the olive oil in a bowl and add the thyme and parsley.

2 Add the chilli powder along with the ground cumin, paprika and a little pepper. Mix everything together thoroughly.

3 Cut the pork into 2 cm x 2 cm cubes. Add the pork cubes to the spice mixture and stir. Cover and leave to marinate overnight in the fridge.

4 The next day, remove the meat from the marinade and thread onto the soaked wooden skewers. Pre-heat the grill. Place the marinade in a pot and bring to a boil.

5 Roast the kebabs on the grill for approx. 5–10 minutes, basting regularly with the marinade.

Grilled steaks
with tomatoes and garlic

Serves 4

1 onion

1 garlic clove

1 red pepper

700 g tomatoes

1 tbsp freshly chopped flat parsley

4 tbsp olive oil

1 tsp dried oregano

1 tsp sugar

salt

pepper

4 rump steaks (160 g each)

Preparation time: approx.
25 minutes (plus cooking and
grilling time)
Per serving approx. 491 kcal/
2053 kJ
37 g P, 31 g F, 12 g CH

1 Peel the onion and garlic. Wash the pepper. Score the tomatoes with a cross and remove the stalks. Scald with boiling water, peel, deseed and dice. Finely chop the pepper, onion, parsley and garlic, and put in a large saucepan with 3 tbsp olive oil, oregano and sugar. Season to taste with salt and pepper. Bring to the boil, reduce the heat and simmer for 15 minutes.

2 In the meantime, wash the meat and pat it dry thoroughly. Season generously with pepper and brush on the remaining olive oil. Sear each side for about 1 minute under a pre-heated grill. Then, on a lower heat, cook according to taste.

3 Put the steaks on warmed plates and pour the sauce on top. Serve immediately with fresh white bread and a mixed salad.

Chicken legs
Andalusian-style

Serves 4

1 onion

4 garlic cloves

2 tbsp raisins

200 ml dry sherry

1 kg chicken legs

salt

black pepper

½ tsp ground cumin

4 tbsp olive oil

1 cinnamon stick

50 g sliced almonds

pinch of ground cinnamon
   (optional)

Preparation time: 15 minutes
(plus cooking time)
Per serving approx. 560 kcal/
2340 kJ
37 g P, 38 g F, 4 g CH

1 Peel and finely chop the onion and garlic. Place the raisins in a bowl, pour over 3 tablespoons of sherry and leave to stand for 10 minutes. Wash the chicken legs in cold water and pat dry. Rub salt, pepper and cumin into the skin.

2 Heat the olive oil in a casserole dish and sweat the onion with the garlic. Add the chicken legs and brown on all sides. Deglaze the dish with the sherry, then break the cinnamon stick in half and drop into the cooking liquid. Cover and simmer over a low heat for approx. 45 minutes.

3 10 minutes before the cooking time is up, add the raisins and almond flakes to the chicken legs, mix well and add salt, pepper, cumin and cinnamon to taste. Remove the cinnamon stick before serving. Place the chicken legs on plates and decorate with flaked almonds and the crumbled cinnamon stick. This dish works well with rice.

Duck legs
in a fruity sauce

Serves 4

4–6 duck legs

salt

pepper

1 onion

4 garlic cloves

2 carrots

1 orange

1 tbsp clarified butter

1 tsp flour

1 bay leaf

1 dried chilli

500 ml dry white wine

175 g green olives

sugar

1 tbsp wine vinegar

Preparation time: 25 minutes
(plus roasting time)
Per serving approx. 558 kcal/
2342 kJ
28 g P, 40 g F, 13 g CH

1 Pre-heat the oven to 225 °C (Gas Mark 7, fan oven 200 °C). Rub salt and pepper into the duck legs. Peel and finely chop the onion and garlic. Peel and slice the carrots. Wash the orange with hot water, dry and cut into slices.

2 Sear the duck legs in the hot clarified butter. Add the onion, garlic and carrot and fry briefly. Sprinkle everything with flour. Add the bay leaf, chilli and orange slices. Roast in the pre-heated oven at 200 °C (Gas Mark 6, fan oven 180 °C) for approx. 20 minutes until crispy. Pour in the wine and cook for another 20 minutes.

3 Pit and slice the olives. Remove the bay leaf, chilli and orange slices from the casserole dish. Boil the sauce down to ⅓ of its original volume and warm the olives in the sauce. Season with salt, pepper, sugar and vinegar. Serve the duck legs with the sauce.

Moussaka

aubergine and lamb bake

Serves 4

3 aubergines

salt

1 onion

1 garlic clove

125 ml olive oil

400 g minced lamb

pepper

400 g chopped tinned
tomatoes

2 tbsp tomato purée

½ tsp ground cinnamon

2 tbsp freshly chopped
parsley

2 tsp finely chopped mint

3 tbsp butter, plus extra for
greasing

3 tbsp flour

300 ml milk

75 g Alpine cheese

Preparation time: 30 minutes
(plus cooking time)
Per serving approx. 570 kcal/
2386 kJ
41 g P, 39 g F, 15 g CH

1 Cut the aubergines into ½ cm thick slices, sprinkle with salt and leave to stand for 1 hour. Chop the onion and garlic clove finely and fry thoroughly in 2 tablespoons of oil along with the minced lamb. Season with salt and pepper. Add the tomatoes with their juice to the meat, stir in the tomato purée, fold in the herbs and spices, then remove the pan from the heat.

2 Rinse the aubergine slices, pat dry and fry on both sides in lots of oil in batches. Place alternating layers of aubergine slices and lamb sauce in a greased casserole dish. Finish with a layer of aubergine slices.

3 Make a roux out of melted butter and flour, add milk and boil down to form a smooth sauce. Season and pour over the contents of the casserole dish. Scatter over the grated cheese and bake for approx. 45 minutes in the oven at 220 °C (Gas Mark 7, fan oven 200 °C).

Coq au vin
the French national dish

Serves 4

1 ready-to-cook chicken
(approx. 1.3 kg)

salt

black pepper

1 tsp sweet paprika

3 shallots

2 garlic cloves

3 carrots

4 tomatoes

300 g small mushrooms

2 tbsp butter

80 g chopped streaky bacon

50 ml Cognac

1 tbsp flour

600 ml dry red wine

½ bunch flat-leaf
parsley, finely chopped

Preparation time: 20 minutes
(plus cooking time)
Per serving approx. 700 kcal/
2930 kJ
48 g P, 41 g F, 15 g CH

1 Rinse the chicken with cold water and pat dry. Divide into 6 to 8 portions using poultry scissors. Rub the inside and outside with salt, pepper and a little paprika.

2 Peel and very finely chop the shallots and garlic. Wash and peel the carrots. Cut into strips lengthways, and then dice. Score crosses into the tomatoes, blanch in boiling water, refresh in cold water, then skin with a small kitchen knife, cut into quarters, deseed and remove the cores. Cut the flesh into cubes. Rub the mushrooms clean with kitchen paper.

3 Melt the butter in a stew pot, add the chopped bacon and fry. Add the mushrooms and fry on all sides, then remove the bacon and mushrooms from the pot and set to one side.

4 Place the chicken pieces in the pot and brown on all sides. Pour in the Cognac and set fire to it with a match. Add the vegetables once the flame has gone out, coat with flour and deglaze with red wine. Cover the pot and braise over a low heat for an hour.

5 In the last 5 minutes of cooking, return the mushrooms and fried bacon to the coq au vin to warm through. Season everything with salt, pepper and paprika and scatter over the parsley. Serve the coq au vin with fresh French bread or potato dumplings.

Lamb ragù
with mushrooms

Serves 4

1 kg boneless leg of lamb

500 g button mushrooms

200 g onions

3 tbsp olive oil

125 ml dry white wine

salt

pepper

1 tbsp freshly chopped
  rosemary

2 tbsp Marsala

Preparation time: 25 minutes
(plus braising and cooking time)
Per serving approx. 452 kcal/
1900 kJ
56 g P, 13 g F, 5 g CH

1 Cut the lamb into cubes. Clean the mushrooms by rubbing them with a damp thumb. Peel the onions and chop roughly.

2 Pre-heat the oven to 190 °C (Gas Mark 5, fan oven 170 °C). Heat the olive oil in a pot and brown the meat thoroughly. Sauté the onions in the pot. Add the mushrooms and wine, and fill with enough water to completely cover the meat. Season with salt, pepper and rosemary.

3 Cover the pot and cook the ragù in the oven for approx. an hour, until the meat is completely tender. Add Marsala to taste.

Fish and seafood

Swordfish
in vegetable and saffron sauce

Serves 4

4 swordfish steaks
salt
pepper
juice of 2 lemons
120 g flour
6 tbsp olive oil
1 onion
2 carrots
100 g celeriac
1 leek
200 ml dry white wine
150 ml cream
pinch of ground saffron
2 tbsp freshly chopped dill

Preparation time: 20 minutes
Per serving approx. 555 kcal/
2324 kJ
37 g P, 26 g F, 33 g CH

1 Add salt and pepper to the swordfish steaks and marinate in the lemon juice. Coat in 100 g of flour and fry for approx. 3 minutes on each side in hot olive oil. Remove from the pan and keep warm.

2 Peel and dice the onion, carrots and celeriac. Slice the leek into rings.

3 Sauté the vegetables in the cooking fat for 5 minutes. Sprinkle over the rest of the flour. Pour in the white wine and cream, add the saffron and let the sauce boil down a little. Season with salt and pepper, and serve with the cooked swordfish steaks. Scatter over the chopped dill.

Baked trout
with olives

Serves 4

4 ready-to-cook trout, 275 g
    each
75 ml olive oil
4 bay leaves
salt
pepper
4 slices pancetta
2 shallots
1 bunch of flat-leaf parsley
120 ml white wine
24 green olives, stoned

Preparation time: approx.
15 minutes (plus baking time)
Per serving approx. 835 kcal/
3507 kJ
59 g P, 64 g F, 3 g CH

1 Wash the trout and pat them dry. Pre-heat the oven to 200 °C (Gas Mark 6, fan oven 180 °C). Trim 4 large pieces of baking parchment to size to wrap the trout in. Grease the parchment with oil.

2 Place 1 trout on each piece of paper. Place a bay leaf in the cavity of each fish and season them with salt and pepper. Wrap each fish in a slice of pancetta.

3 Peel and chop the shallots. Wash the parsley, shake dry and chop. Sprinkle the shallots and parsley on the trout and carefully pour on the wine. Place the olives on top and close up the paper packages tightly around the trout so that liquid cannot escape.

4 Place the wrapped trout on a baking tray in the oven and bake for 25 minutes. Place the trout packages on plates and unwrap at the table.

Oven-baked sea bream
with herbs

Serves 4

1 large, ready-to-cook sea bream

4 bay leaves

1 bunch parsley

1 sprig thyme

a few tarragon leaves

a few sprigs basil

butter for greasing

135 ml olive oil

salt

pepper

flour

fresh herbs for garnishing

Preparation time: 30 minutes
(plus standing and roasting time)
Per serving approx. 475 kcal/
1989 kJ
32 g P, 38 g F, 3 g CH

1 Wash the fish and pat dry thoroughly. Put the bay leaves and ⅓ of the washed and dried herbs in a greased baking dish, stuff the fish with some of the herbs, place it in the baking dish and cover with the rest of the herbs. Pour over 45 ml of olive oil and leave to stand in a cool place for approx. 1 hour. Remove the fish from the baking dish and pat dry.

2 Season the fish with salt and pepper, then coat in flour.

3 Heat the rest of the olive oil in another baking dish and flash-fry the fish on both sides. Place in the oven and roast for approx. 35–40 minutes at 200 °C (Gas Mark 6, fan oven 180 °C), basting several times with the herb oil. The fish is ready when the dorsal fin can be pulled out easily. Serve garnished with fresh herbs.

Squid stew
with olives

Serves 4

600 g ready-to-cook squid
  with tentacles

2 onions

1 garlic clove

4 tbsp olive oil

400 g tomato passata

100 g pitted green olives

2 tbsp capers

500 ml fish stock

200 ml white wine

salt

pepper

pinch of sugar

4 tomatoes

1 bunch tarragon

Preparation time: 30 minutes
(plus cooking time)
Per serving approx. 310 kcal/
1298 kJ
29 g P, 12 g F, 13 g CH

1 Wash the squid and cut into small pieces. Peel and chop the onions and garlic. Sauté the squid in hot olive oil, then add the onion and garlic and fry. Stir in the tomato passata. Chop and add the olives and capers, pour in the stock and wine, and season with salt, pepper and sugar. Cover and leave to simmer for approx. 1 hour.

2 Skin, deseed and dice the fresh tomatoes and chop the tarragon. Stir into the sauce, heat through and serve with bread.

Stuffed mussels
with tomatoes

Serves 4

1.5 kg mussels

5 eggs

250 g breadcrumbs

125 g freshly grated
Pecorino

3 tbsp freshly chopped
parsley

1 garlic clove

3 tbsp olive oil

400 g tomato passata

salt

pepper

1 tbsp freshly chopped
oregano

Preparation time: 30 minutes
(plus baking and cooking time)
Per serving approx. 768 kcal/
3224 kJ
60 g P, 30 g F, 64 g CH

1 Wash the mussels thoroughly under running water and discard any that are open. Pre-heat the oven to 200 °C (Gas Mark 6, fan oven 180 °C). Bring water to a boil in a large pot and cook the mussels for approx. 5 minutes until they open. Throw away any that do not open. Drain the mussels and leave to dry.

2 Whisk the eggs and mix with the breadcrumbs and cheese. Fold in the parsley and beat until creamy. Place the opened mussels on a baking tray and divide the egg mixture between them. Carefully close the mussel shells and bake the mussels in the oven for approx. 15 minutes.

3 Peel and finely chop the garlic for the sauce. Heat the oil in a pot and fry the garlic. Add the tomatoes and simmer the mixture over a medium heat for approx. 10 minutes. Add salt, pepper and oregano to taste.

Gilthead bream fillets
with broad beans

Serves 4

8 gilthead bream fillets with skin

salt

pepper

6 tbsp olive oil

250 g freshly picked broad beans

3 tomatoes

2 tbsp freshly chopped parsley

2 tbsp Vin Santo

1 handful of basil leaves

Preparation time: approx. 20 minutes (plus frying and cooking time)
Per serving approx. 630 kcal/ 2646 kJ
86 g P, 23 g F, 19 g CH

1 Pre-heat the oven to 200 °C (Gas Mark 6, fan oven 180 °C). Wash and pat dry the fish and rub in salt and pepper. Grease an ovenproof dish with 2 tbsp oil. Place the fillets in the dish, skin side up, and bake in the oven for 5 minutes.

2 Remove the beans from their inner skin and halve. Cook in salted boiling water for 10 minutes. Pour off the water and drain.

3 Score the tomatoes with a cross, scald with boiling water, remove the skins, stalks and seeds, and dice the flesh. Mix together the beans and tomatoes and then stir in salt, pepper and parsley.

4 Heat the remaining olive oil and toss the tomato and bean mixture in it whilst stirring for 3 minutes. Deglaze with Vin Santo. Put the vegetables on plates and arrange the fish fillets on top. Serve garnished with basil leaves.

Fish stew
with fruits de mer

Serves 4–6

1 kg fish and mixed seafood
(e.g. squid, whiting, bream,
prawns, mussels, clams)

200 ml olive oil

5 garlic cloves

1 dried red chilli pepper

500 ml white wine

800 g tinned, peeled
tomatoes

1 onion

1 carrot

2 sticks celery

½ bunch parsley

juice of 1 lemon

salt

pepper

Cayenne pepper

Preparation time: approx.
40 minutes (plus cooking time)
Per serving approx. 903 kcal/
3793 kJ
36 g P, 66 g F, 23 g CH

1 Wash the fish and seafood, brush the mussels. Cut the large fish into pieces, leaving the smaller fish whole. Put half the quantity of oil in a large pan and heat. Peel the garlic cloves and fry whole in the hot oil. Crumble the chilli pepper into the pan and fry. Add the cleaned squid. After 5 minutes, pour on 400 ml wine and add the tomatoes, including their juice. Simmer everything for 30 minutes.

2 Heat the remaining oil in a second saucepan. Peel the onion and carrot, wash the celery. Dice the vegetables. Wash the parsley, shake dry and chop. Sauté the vegetables and parsley in the oil. Add the lemon juice, fish and fish pieces. Cook for about 10 minutes, then remove the fish. Remove the fish from the bones and put to one side. Place the bones back in the pan, add the remaining wine and a little water, and simmer, covered, for 20 minutes.

3 Pass the stock through a sieve. Pour into the saucepan and cook the mussels in it until all the shells have opened (throw away the unopened ones).

4 Remove the squid from the tomato stock, cut into rings and add to the mussels. Pass the tomato stock through a sieve, pour onto the mussels and squid, and then add the fish. Season with salt, pepper and spicy Cayenne pepper. Serve in bowls and with garlic bread.

Mediterranean
fish skewers

Serves 4

40 g cod fillet

8 shelled tiger prawns

1 courgette

8 wooden skewers

12 cherry tomatoes

1 garlic clove

4 tbsp olive oil

salt

pepper

1 tsp Italian mixed herbs

Preparation time: 15 minutes
(plus grilling time)
Per serving approx. 236 kcal/
991 kJ
38 g P, 7 g F, 3 g CH

1 Wash the fish fillets, pat dry and cut into bite-sized pieces. Remove any tendons from the prawns. Wash the courgette and cut into 1 cm thick slices. Thread the ingredients onto the wooden skewers together with the cherry tomatoes.

2 Peel and crush the garlic clove. Make a marinade out of garlic, olive oil, salt, pepper and the Italian herbs, and brush it over the fish skewers.

3 Place the skewers on a baking tray covered in aluminium foil and grill for approx. 8 minutes under a grill heated to 250 °C (Gas Mark 10). Turn the skewers several times and baste occasionally with the marinade.

Gilthead sea bream
with porcini mushrooms

Serves 4

2 ready-to-cook gilthead sea bream

salt

1 tbsp lemon juice

10 tbsp olive oil

100 g porcini mushrooms

50 g flaked almonds

4 tbsp Vin Santo

½ tsp freshly chopped thyme

Preparation time: approx.
20 minutes (plus cooking time)
Per serving approx. 313 kcal/
1313 kJ
17 g P, 26 g F, 2 g CH

1 Pre-heat the oven to 180 °C (Gas Mark 4, fan oven 160 °C). Wash the fish, pat dry, salt inside and out, then drizzle with lemon juice. Place the fish on two adequately sized pieces of aluminium foil and drizzle with 3 tbsp olive oil.

2 Clean the mushrooms, wipe with a damp cloth and slice thinly. Toast the almond flakes dry. Add the mushrooms and almonds to the fish.

3 Season everything with salt, drizzle the remaining olive oil and wine on top, sprinkle with thyme and close the foil parcel. Bake in the oven for about 25 minutes.

4 Serve the fish in the foil, opening the parcels at the table. Serve with fresh bread.

Bulgur-stuffed gilthead sea bream

Serves 4

60 g bulgur wheat

4 shallots

1 stick celery

3 garlic cloves

vegetable oil

½ bunch chopped parsley

1 tbsp freshly chopped dill

½ tsp salt

freshly ground pepper

4 ready-to-cook gilthead sea bream

1 lime, cut into quarters

Preparation time: 30 minutes
(plus soaking and cooking time)
Per serving approx. 367 kcal/
1536 kJ
50 g P, 13 g F, 10 g CH

1 Soak the bulgur wheat in approx. 100 ml of boiling water and leave to stand for 20 minutes, until the water has been absorbed.

2 Pre-heat the oven to 180 °C (Gas Mark 4, fan oven 160 °C). Peel and chop the shallots. Wash and chop the celery. Peel and slice the garlic.

3 Heat a little vegetable oil in a pan and fry the vegetables and the garlic over a medium heat for approx. 5 minutes, until the chopped shallots are translucent. Remove the pan from the stove and stir in the bulgur wheat, parsley, dill, salt and pepper.

4 Wash the sea bream thoroughly and rub dry. Stuff each fish with a quarter of the bulgur mixture. Place the fish on a baking tray covered with baking parchment and bake for approx. 30 minutes. The fish is ready when it can be crushed with a fork.

5 Remove the skins from the fish and sprinkle with ground pepper. Serve garnished with the lime quarters.

Pepper-stuffed
sardines

Serves 4

2 red peppers
125 g butter
1 kg fresh sardines
sea salt
4 tbsp olive oil
2 tbsp breadcrumbs

Preparation time: 30 minutes
(plus cooking time)
Per serving approx. 570 kcal/
2394 kJ
50 g P, 39 g F, 6 g CH

1 Wash and halve the peppers and cut into thin strips.

2 Melt 80 g butter in a pan and fry the pepper strips gently until they are soft.

3 Clean the sardines and carefully remove the spines and guts. Wash the fish carefully and leave to dry.

4 Pre-heat the oven to 180 °C (Gas Mark 4, fan oven 160 °C). Sprinkle the sardines with sea salt, stuff with some of the pepper strips and press together firmly.

5 Pack the sardines tightly in an ovenproof dish, place the rest of the pepper strips on top and pour over the olive oil.

6 Sprinkle the breadcrumbs. Dab the rest of the butter on top and bake in the oven for approx. 15–20 minutes.

Tomato cod
with potatoes

Serves 4

700 g dried cod
250 g potatoes
salt
4 rosemary sprigs
½ bunch of parsley
4 garlic cloves
600 g tomatoes
275 ml olive oil
150 ml white wine
pepper
sugar to taste
3 tbsp plain flour

Preparation time: approx.
30 minutes (plus soaking, braising
and cooking time)
Per serving approx.
1115 kcal/4683 kJ
137 g P, 40 g F, 24 g CH

1 Soak the dried cod in cold water for 24 hours, changing the water two or three times. Remove the fish from the water, drain and put in a saucepan. Cover with cold water and bring to the boil. Then pour off the water, let the fish drain and cut into bite-sized pieces.

2 Peel and halve the potatoes and cook until soft in a little salted water. Wash the herbs, shake dry and chop. Peel the garlic and chop. Scald the tomatoes with boiling water, remove the skins, stalks and seeds, and dice. Heat 2 tablespoons of oil in a saucepan and sauté the garlic. Add the tomatoes, pour on the wine and season to taste with salt, pepper and sugar. Simmer for 25 minutes.

3 Heat the remaining oil in a saucepan. Put the flour on a plate with a little pepper. Toss the fish pieces in the flour, brush off the excess and fry in hot oil until golden brown. Drain on kitchen paper. Add the fish pieces to the cooked potatoes in the tomato sauce and allow to steep for a short time. Serve.

Galician squid
with king prawns

Serves 4

1 medium waxy potato
salt
300 g squid
175 g king prawns
3–5 tbsp olive oil
2 garlic cloves
1 tomato
pepper

Preparation time: 30 minutes
Per serving approx. 180 kcal/
757 kJ
22 g P, 5 g F, 10 g CH

1 Peel and wash the potato, cook in salted water for approx. 20 minutes, leave to cool a little, then cut into slices and place in a bowl. Wash the squid and slice into thin rings.

2 Peel and devein the prawns. Wash and leave to dry. Sprinkle with salt. Heat 2 tablespoons of oil, peel the garlic and sauté gently in the hot oil with the prawns and squid rings until the prawns are pink. Add to the bowl with the potato.

3 Scald the tomato with boiling water for 30 seconds, then skin and cut in half, remove the core and seeds, and dice finely. Scatter the tomato pieces over the ingredients in the bowl and mix everything carefully together.

4 Heat the rest of the olive oil until very hot and pour over the ingredients. Sprinkle with salt and pepper, mix together, arrange in bowls and serve with bread.

Baked prawns
with saffron mayonnaise

Serves 4

500 g ready-to-cook prawns

2 garlic cloves

75 ml olive oil

2 tbsp lemon juice

salt

2 egg yolks

pinch of ground saffron

approx. 200 ml sunflower oil

pepper

Preparation time: 15 minutes
(plus cooking time)
Per serving approx. 560 kcal/
2352 kJ
28 g P, 50 g F, 3 g CH

1 Pre-heat the oven to 175 °C (Gas Mark 3, fan oven 150 °C). Peel the prawns, but do not remove the tails. Wash and dry the prawns. Peel and finely chop the garlic.

2 Mix the olive oil, garlic, 1 tablespoon of lemon juice and salt together well. Add the prawns and mix thoroughly. Finally, put everything in a *cazuela* (cast-iron or stainless steel pot). Bake in the oven for approx. 20 minutes.

3 While the prawns are cooking, mix the egg yolks thoroughly with the ground saffron, salt and 1 tablespoon of lemon juice. Stir in the sunflower oil drop by drop to begin with, then in a thin stream. Season with salt and pepper. Serve the baked prawns with the saffron mayonnaise and toasted bread.

Mussels
with chilli and vegetables

Serves 4

5 onions
60 g ham
1 small red jalapeño pepper
2 tbsp olive oil
1 tbsp medium sherry
60 small ready-to-cook
   Venus mussels

Preparation time: 30 minutes
(plus cooking time)
Per serving approx. 170 kcal/
710 kJ
21 g P, 4 g F, 13 g CH

1 Peel the onions and slice into very thin rings. Cut the ham into tiny cubes. Wash, halve and finely dice the jalapeño.

2 Heat the olive oil, add the onions, cover and fry for 10 minutes until they are translucent.

3 Stir in the ham and jalapeño, pour in the sherry and add the mussels.

4 Place the lid on the pan and simmer for a few minutes over a low heat until the mussels open.

5 Remove the mussels, discard any that have not opened, and put the rest of the mussels back in the broth. Serve the mussels with their broth.

Salads and vegetables

Greek salad
a rustic mix

Serves 4

1 cucumber

2 yellow peppers

500 g tomatoes

2 spring onions

120 g black olives

200 g feta cheese

½ bunch flat-leaf parsley

6 sprigs thyme

1 garlic clove

4 tbsp white wine vinegar

6 tbsp olive oil

salt

black pepper

Preparation time: 30 minutes
Per serving approx. 420 kcal/
1760 kJ
12 g P, 36 g F, 12 g CH

1 Wash and peel the cucumber and cut in half lengthways. Cut into ½ cm thick pieces. Wash and halve the peppers, remove the membranes and seeds, and cut into cubes. Wash and halve the tomatoes, remove the cores and cut into eighths.

2 Wash the spring onions, remove the roots and the withered green outer parts and slice into very thin rings. Drain the olives and crumble the feta using your hands. Wash the parsley and pat dry. Tear the leaves from their stalks and chop finely. Mix all of the prepared ingredients together in a large salad bowl.

3 To make the dressing, wash the thyme and pat dry. Strip the leaves from their stalks. Peel the garlic and chop very finely using a large kitchen knife. Mix together the vinegar, olive oil, thyme and garlic. Season with salt and pepper and add to the salad mixture. Pitta bread makes a good accompaniment.

Salade niçoise
with artichokes

Serves 4

4 eggs
600 g tomatoes
1 cucumber
2 yellow peppers
4 spring onions
1 garlic clove
8 preserved artichokes
140 g canned tuna
8 anchovy fillets
1 sprig lemon thyme
2 sprigs basil
4 tbsp olive oil
2 tbsp red wine vinegar
salt
black pepper
80 g black olives
1 tbsp capers (from a jar)

Preparation time: 50 minutes
(plus cooking time)
Per serving approx. 430 kcal/
1800 kJ
21 g P, 30 g F, 15 g CH

1 Hard-boil the eggs, plunge in cold water, peel and then leave to cool. Cut into slices.

2 Wash the vegetables and pat dry. Halve the tomatoes, remove the stalks and cut into eighths. Peel the cucumber using a potato peeler and slice thinly. Halve the peppers and remove the cores, membranes and seeds. Cut the flesh into narrow strips. Wash the spring onions, remove the roots and the withered outer green parts and slice into very thin rings. Peel the garlic and chop finely with a large knife.

3 Remove the artichokes from the jar, drain well and cut in half. Drain the tuna and flake with a fork. Rinse the anchovy fillets with cold water, pat dry with kitchen paper and cut in half.

4 Wash the herbs and pat dry. Tear the thyme leaves from their stems. Do the same with the basil and chop finely.

5 Mix the oil with the red wine vinegar to make a marinade. Season with salt and pepper.

6 Arrange the salad on 4 large plates, then spoon the herbs, olives and capers over the top and drizzle with the marinade.

Panzanella
Italian bread salad

Serves 4

150 g stale white bread

125 ml vegetable stock

1 onion

1 garlic clove

200 g tomatoes

200 g cucumber

1 bunch basil

2 tbsp white balsamic vinegar

4 tbsp olive oil

salt

pepper

2 tbsp freshly shaved Parmesan

Preparation time: 20 minutes
Per serving approx. 173 kcal/ 724 kJ
5 g P, 7 g F, 22 g CH

1 Cut the bread into cubes and soak in the cold vegetable stock for 15 minutes. Peel and finely chop the onion and garlic. Skin, deseed and dice the tomatoes. Peel and dice the cucumber. Wash the basil, shake dry and slice, keeping back a few leaves for garnishing.

2 Make a dressing out of the white balsamic vinegar, oil, salt and pepper. Remove the bread from the stock. Mix with the other ingredients, pour over the dressing and sprinkle with Parmesan.

Apulian
rice salad

Serves 4

300 g rice

salt

2 carrots

1 red pepper

1 bunch spring onions

100 ml white balsamic
  vinegar

1 tsp sugar

150 g peas (frozen)

50 g each of green and black
  olives

150 g tinned tuna

1 lemon

2 tbsp olive oil

½ bunch of parsley

Preparation time: approx.
40 minutes (plus steeping time)
Per serving approx. 330 kcal/
1382 kJ
12 g P, 9 g F, 49 g CH

1 Cook the rice according to the packet instructions in salted water for 15 minutes. Drain and allow to cool. Wash and peel the carrots and dice finely. Deseed and wash the pepper and cut into fine strips. Wash the spring onions and cut into fine rings.

2 Bring to the boil 50 ml water, the balsamic vinegar and the sugar. Add the carrots and cook for 4 minutes. Then add the peas and bring to the boil again. Add the pepper and spring onions and allow to cool in the vinegar broth.

3 Stone the olives and chop finely. Drain the tuna and loosen with a fork. Juice the lemon. Drain the vegetables, reserve the broth and mix with the lemon juice and salt. Beat in the olive oil with a fork. Wash the parsley, shake dry and chop finely.

4 Mix rice, vegetables, olives, tuna, parsley and dressing, allowing the salad to steep for at least 1 hour before serving.

Courgettes
with tomatoes and basil

Serves 4

500 g tomatoes

500 g courgettes

2 garlic cloves

2 shallots

1 bunch basil

3 tbsp olive oil

1 tbsp pine nuts

salt

pepper

Preparation time: 30 minutes
Per serving approx. 94 kcal/394 kJ
4 g P, 5 g F, 7 g CH

1 Scald the tomatoes with hot water, skin, deseed and cut into cubes. Dice the courgettes. Peel and chop the garlic and shallots. Wash the basil, shake dry and chop.

2 Heat the oil and fry the shallots and garlic until translucent. Add the pine nuts, tomatoes and courgettes and fry, stirring often. Add the basil, season with salt and pepper and leave to stand for another 15 minutes. Toasted white bread makes a good accompaniment to this salad.

Stuffed tomatoes
with olives

Serves 4

8 medium-sized tomatoes
(or 4 large tomatoes)

1 onion

2 garlic cloves

4 tbsp olive oil

75 g black olives

1 tbsp capers

1 tbsp chopped sunflower
seeds

1 bunch basil

salt

pepper

4 tbsp breadcrumbs

30 g Parmesan

oil for the baking tin

Preparation time: 20 minutes
(plus baking time)
Per serving approx. 202 kcal/
846 kJ
5 g P, 16 g F, 9 g CH

1 Cut the top off each of the tomatoes to form a lid, remove the seeds with a spoon. Cut the flesh removed from the middle and the lid into small dice. Chop the onion and garlic cloves and sauté in 1 tablespoon of olive oil. Add the flesh from the tomatoes, the pitted and chopped olives, the drained capers, the sunflower seeds and the chopped basil and fry for approx. 5 minutes. Add salt and pepper.

2 Fry the breadcrumbs in 1 tablespoon of oil, then stir in 1 tablespoon of grated Parmesan. Stir half of this mixture into the vegetables and stuff into the hollowed-out tomatoes.

3 Place the tomatoes in a greased baking tin, scatter over the rest of the breadcrumb mixture and the rest of the cheese and drizzle with 2 tablespoons of olive oil. Bake in the oven for approx. 25 minutes at 200 °C (Gas Mark 6, fan oven 180 °C).

Vegetable casserole
with potatoes

Serves 4

300 g tomatoes

2 green peppers

2 aubergines

500 g potatoes

5 tbsp olive oil

250 g mozzarella

200 ml dry white wine

200 ml vegetable stock

salt

pepper

2 tbsp breadcrumbs

freshly chopped thyme

1 bunch basil

Preparation time: 20 minutes
(plus cooking time)
Per serving approx. 413 kcal/
1729 kJ
18 g P, 20 g F, 30 g CH

1 Cut the tomatoes, peppers and aubergines into thin slices or strips. Peel and slice the potatoes.

2 Brush an ovenproof dish with olive oil. Arrange the vegetables in the dish in alternating layers.

3 Slice the mozzarella and lay over the top. Pour over the wine and stock. Season with salt and pepper. Mix the breadcrumbs with the thyme and scatter over the dish. Bake for approx. an hour in the oven at 200 °C (Gas Mark 6, fan oven 180 °C). Cut the basil into strips and scatter over the casserole before serving.

Cottage potatoes
with herby oil

Serves 4

500 g waxy potatoes

coarse sea salt

1 garlic clove

10 stalks flat parsley

60 ml olive oil

salt

freshly ground black pepper

Preparation time: approx.
20 minutes (plus cooking time)
Per serving approx. 253 kcal/
1058 kJ
3 g P, 15 g F, 25 g CH

1 Wash the potatoes and cook in salted water. Peel the garlic and chop finely. Wash the parsley and shake it dry; remove the leaves from the stalks and chop. Mix the garlic and the parsley with olive oil and season with salt and pepper.

2 Drain the potatoes, peel immediately and cut into cubes 2–3 cm in size. Add the potatoes to the other ingredients whilst still hot, mix carefully and serve warm or cold. Cottage potatoes go well with grilled fish and a fresh, mixed salad.

Vegetable frittata
with Parmesan

Serves 4

200 g carrots
3 shallots
400 g courgettes
1 tbsp olive oil
1 garlic clove
1 tbsp rosemary
80 g Parmesan
4 eggs
3 tbsp cream
salt
pepper
oil for the baking dish

Preparation time: 25 minutes
(plus cooking time)
Per serving approx. 182 kcal/
764 kJ
11 g P, 12 g F, 5 g CH

1 Peel the carrots and shallots, wash the courgettes and grate all three vegetables. Heat the olive oil in a pan and sauté the vegetables for 2 minutes. Peel the garlic clove and crush it into the pan. Stir in the rosemary. Sauté everything for another minute.

2 Pre-heat the oven to 200 °C (Gas Mark 6, fan oven 180 °C). Grate 2 tablespoons of Parmesan. Mix the eggs with the cream and Parmesan, and season with salt and pepper.

3 Spoon the vegetables into a greased round baking dish, pour over the egg and cream mixture, and bake in the oven for approx. 20 minutes. Before serving, cut into wedges and scatter over Parmesan shavings.

Braised artichokes
with fresh mint

Serves 4

8 young artichokes
(approx. 600 g)

salt

pepper

2 garlic cloves

4 tbsp olive oil

125 ml dry white wine

1 tbsp lemon juice

fresh mint

Preparation time: 20 minutes
(plus braising and cooking time)
Per serving approx. 83 kcal/
352 kJ
4 g P, 3 g F, 6 g CH

1 Wash the artichokes, cut off the stalks and remove the outer leaves. Cut off the hard tips of the remaining leaves with scissors. Season the artichokes with salt and pepper.

2 Peel and finely chop the garlic. Heat the oil in a large pan and sauté the garlic for 2 minutes. Add the artichokes to the pan and cook over a medium heat for another 2 minutes until they are golden brown.

3 Pour in the wine, cover the pan and cook the artichokes for approx. 30 minutes, until they are tender and have a good colour. Add more wine if necessary.

4 Remove the artichokes from the pan and drizzle with lemon juice. Serve immediately with the fresh mint leaves and bread.

Caponata
Sicilian vegetables

Serves 4

2 Spanish onions

2 red onions

6 tomatoes

2 red and 2 yellow peppers

4 courgettes

2 aubergines

6 tbsp olive oil

2 tbsp honey

2 tbsp balsamic vinegar

salt

pepper

Preparation time: approx.
25 minutes (plus cooking time)
Per serving approx. 234 kcal/
973 kJ
6 g P, 11 g F, 25 g CH

1 Peel the onions and cut into rings. Score the tomatoes with a cross and remove the stalks. Then scald with boiling water, peel, deseed and dice.

2 Clean and wash the remaining vegetables, and slice or cut into strips, as preferred. Then brown the onions in hot olive oil. Add peppers, courgettes, aubergines and tomatoes (in that order) at 1–2-minute intervals. Reduce heat and cook for 5–10 minutes.

3 Add honey and balsamic vinegar. Season to taste with salt and pepper. Serve with warm ciabatta.

Aubergine and
mozzarella gratin

Serves 4

800 g medium-sized
  aubergines
salt
300 g mozzarella
½ bunch oregano
½ bunch basil
500 g tinned tomatoes
100 g flour
100 ml olive oil
50 g freshly grated
  Parmesan
oil for the baking dish

Preparation time: 30 minutes
(plus cooking time)
Per serving approx. 445 kcal/
1869 kJ
25 g P, 26 g F, 27 g CH

1 Wash the aubergines, pat dry and cut lengthways into ½ cm thick slices. Place the slices in a bowl, sprinkle with salt and leave to stand for approx. 15 minutes.

2 Pre-heat the oven to 180 °C (Gas Mark 4, fan oven 160 °C). Cut the mozzarella into small cubes. Wash the herbs, shake dry, tear the leaves from their stalks and chop. Put the tomatoes in a bowl and purée using a stick blender. Mix the herbs into the tomato purée.

3 Take the aubergines out of the bowl, rinse and pat dry. Turn the slices in the flour to coat. Heat the olive oil in a pan and fry the slices on both sides until golden brown. Leave to dry on kitchen paper.

4 Grease a baking dish and place alternate layers of aubergine slices, tomato purée and mozzarella in it, finishing off with a layer of tomato purée. Scatter the Parmesan over the top. Bake in the oven for approx. 10 minutes.

Potatoes
with sea salt and aioli

Serves 4

750 g small waxy potatoes
sea salt
3 garlic cloves
approx. 150 g mayonnaise
⅓ bunch parsley

Preparation time: 25 minutes
(plus cooking and baking time)
Per serving approx. 325 kcal/
1365 kJ
5 g P, 21 g F, 29 g CH

1 Scrub and wash the potatoes and place in a pot with generously salted water. Add salt until the potatoes float on the surface of the water. If they sink to the bottom, add more salt. Boil the potatoes for 15–20 minutes.

2 Meanwhile, to make the aioli, peel the garlic, crush and add to the mayonnaise. Wash the parsley, shake dry and chop finely, then add to the mayonnaise and stir.

3 Drain the potatoes, return them to the pot, sprinkle with sea salt and then put the pot back on the stove. Cook over a low heat, shaking the pot constantly, until the salt on the potatoes has crystallised.

4 As soon as the salt has crystallised, turn off the heat, cover the pot with a tea towel and leave to stand for 5 minutes. Serve the potatoes with the aioli.

Ratatouille
French vegetable stew

Serves 4

300 g aubergines
salt
500 g tomatoes
250 g courgettes
1 red pepper
1 green pepper
1 yellow pepper
2 onions
4 garlic cloves
½ bunch basil
4 tbsp olive oil
black pepper
1 sprig of rosemary
½ bunch thyme
½ bunch oregano

Preparation time: 30 minutes
(plus cooking time)
Per serving approx. 170 kcal/
710 kJ
5 g P, 11 g F, 12 g CH

1 Wash the aubergines, rub dry and remove the stalks. Halve lengthways and cut into ½ cm thick slices. Sprinkle with salt and leave to stand for approx. 10 minutes in order to get rid of any bitterness. Rinse with water, pat dry and cut into cubes.

2 Score crosses into the tomatoes, scald briefly with boiling water, then plunge in cold water, skin, cut into quarters, deseed and remove the cores. Cut into cubes. Wash the courgettes and cut into small dice. Wash and halve the peppers and cut the flesh into cubes. Peel and very finely chop the onions and garlic. Wash the basil and pat dry with kitchen paper. Chop the leaves finely with a large kitchen knife.

3 Heat the olive oil in a casserole dish. Fry the aubergine cubes in the oil at a high heat, then remove and set to one side. Do the same with the other vegetables. Leave the onions and garlic to last. Sweat them in the oil, then return the other vegetables to the dish. Season with salt and pepper, place the sprigs of herbs on top, cover and leave the ratatouille to braise over a low heat for approx. 25 minutes. Add a little water if necessary.

4 Serve the ratatouille as an accompaniment to roast meat, rice or French bread.

Pizzas and breads

Flatbreads
with stuffing

Serves 8

600 ml milk

20 g yeast

2 tbsp sugar

1 kg flour

200 ml sunflower oil

1 tsp salt

750 g minced meat or
sheep's cheese

1 egg yolk

butter for spreading

Preparation time: 40 minutes
(plus standing time)
Per serving approx. 1800 kcal/
7560 kJ
69 g P, 86 g F, 187 g CH

1 Warm the milk, mix with the yeast and sugar, and leave to stand for 30 minutes. Stir in the flour, oil and salt to make a smooth dough, then leave to rest for 60 minutes.

2 Meanwhile, prepare the filling: season and fry the minced meat or cut the sheep's cheese into small pieces. Divide the dough into several portions and roll out into oval shapes.

3 Pre-heat the oven to 200 °C (Gas Mark 6, fan oven 180 °C). Place a tablespoon of filling in the middle of each piece of dough and fold the edges inwards so that the filling is completely covered.

4 Fill all of the pieces of dough in the same way. Brush the edges of the dough with whisked egg yolk, place the flatbreads on a baking tray and bake in the oven for 20 minutes until golden brown. Spread with butter and serve hot.

Focaccia
with olives

Makes 1 round pizza

275 g flour

½ tsp salt

1 tsp dried yeast

7 tbsp olive oil

12 large green olives

Preparation time: 20 minutes
(plus resting and baking time)
Per pizza approx. 520 kcal/2177 kJ
29 g P, 31 g F, 52 g CH

1 Make a yeast dough from the flour, salt, dried yeast, 175 ml of warm water and 2 tablespoons of olive oil. Knead the dough thoroughly and lay in a round pizza pan, greased with 1 tablespoon of oil. Press the dough until it is 2 cm thick. Cover and leave to prove for 30 minutes.

2 Halve and deseed the olives. Using your fingers, make small dents in the dough and insert the olives.

3 Salt the dough lightly, then drizzle over the remaining 4 tablespoons of olive oil. Bake the focaccia for 25 minutes in the oven at 200 °C (Gas Mark 6, fan oven 180 °C). Serve hot.

Pizza Bambino
with salami

Serves 4

450 g flour
1 packet dried yeast
pinch of sugar
½ tsp salt
5 tbsp olive oil
1 onion
1 tbsp butter
400 g chunky tinned
   tomatoes
salt
pepper
1 tbsp dried oregano
2 small courgettes
200 g button mushrooms
2 yellow peppers
100 g Italian sliced salami
flour for the worktop
butter for greasing
250 g mozzarella
100 g middle-aged Gouda

Preparation time: 40 minutes
(plus resting and baking time)
Per serving approx. 457 kcal/
1913 kJ
26 g P, 36 g F, 6 g CH

1 Place the flour, yeast and sugar in a bowl, slowly add salt, oil and 500 ml of lukewarm water, and work everything into a smooth dough. Cover and leave to prove in a warm place for approx. 1 hour.

2 Sauté the chopped onion in the warm butter. Deglaze with the juice from the tomatoes, then add the tomato chunks, season with salt, pepper and oregano, and leave the mixture to boil down a little. Slice the courgettes and mushrooms, and cut the peppers and salami into strips.

3 Knead the dough on a floured surface, then roll out onto a greased baking tray and leave to prove for another 10 minutes.

4 Spread the tomato sauce on the dough. Arrange the vegetables, mushrooms and salami strips on top, and season with salt, pepper and oregano. Slice the mozzarella and divide between the pizzas. Scatter with the grated Gouda. Bake in the oven at 220 °C (Gas Mark 7, fan oven 200 °C) for approx. 25 minutes.

Spinach calzone
with ricotta

Serves 4

450 g flour
7 g dried yeast
4 tbsp olive oil
1 onion
2 garlic cloves
300 g spinach
salt
pepper
nutmeg
200 g ricotta
60 g black olives, stoned
4 tbsp tomato purée
2 egg yolks
flour for the work surface

Preparation time: approx.
45 minutes (plus resting and
baking time)
Per serving approx. 743 kcal/
3107 kJ
24 g P, 30 g F, 89 g CH

1 Mix the flour with the dried yeast in a bowl. Add 200 ml lukewarm water and 3 tbsp olive oil, and knead into a smooth dough. Cover and allow the dough to prove in a warm place for 45 minutes until it has doubled in size.

2 Heat the remaining olive oil in a frying pan. Peel the onion and garlic, chop into small pieces and sear in the hot oil. Wash the spinach and squeeze out the water. Add to the pan and stew until cooked. Season with salt, pepper and nutmeg.

3 Drain the ricotta, dice and add. Then also add the olives.

4 Divide the dough into 4 portions and roll each one out on a floured surface to form a circle of 20–25 cm in diameter. Spread tomato purée on the dough circles and put some spinach filling in the middle. Fold the dough over so that the filling is covered. Press the edges together well.

5 Allow the dough pockets to prove for another 15 minutes on a baking sheet lined with parchment paper. Brush the calzoni with egg yolk and bake in a pre-heated oven at 210 °C (Gas Mark 6, fan oven 190 °C) for about 20 minutes until golden brown.

Pizza contadina
with spinach and bacon

Makes 1 round pizza

250 g flour
25 g yeast
salt
6 tbsp olive oil
400 g tomatoes
4 onions
4 garlic cloves
pepper
½ tsp sugar
½ tsp dried oregano
½ tsp dried thyme
175 g bacon
250 g spinach
150 g grated Parmesan

Preparation time: 30 minutes
(plus resting and baking time)
Per pizza approx. 853 kcal/
3571 kJ
25 g P, 61 g F, 53 g CH

1 Make a dough out of flour, yeast, 100 ml of luke-warm water, a pinch of salt and 4 tablespoons of olive oil. Leave to prove for 1 hour.

2 Skin, deseed and dice the tomatoes. Peel and chop 2 onions and 2 garlic cloves, and sauté in 1 tablespoon of hot olive oil. Add the tomatoes, season with salt, pepper, sugar, oregano and thyme, and boil down a little until it forms a smooth tomato sauce.

3 Roll out the dough and place in the oiled pizza pan, then spread with the tomato sauce.

4 Peel and dice the remaining onions and garlic. Dice the bacon. Fry until golden brown in a tablespoon of hot olive oil, then sauté the onions and garlic cloves in the fat. Remove from the heat.

5 Cut the spinach into strips and place on the dough, add the bacon and onion mixture on top, and scatter over the cheese. Bake the pizza in the oven at 200 °C (Gas Mark 6, fan oven 180 °C) for approx. 20 minutes.

Pizza Vesuvio
with Gorgonzola

Makes 1 round pizza

250 g flour
25 g fresh yeast
salt
5 tbsp olive oil
400 g tomatoes
2 onions
2 garlic cloves
pepper
½ tsp sugar
½ tsp dried oregano
50 g grated Pecorino
1 red pepper
50 g Gorgonzola
½ red chilli
2 tbsp herb oil

Preparation time: 30 minutes
(plus resting and baking time)
Per pizza approx. 453 kcal/1897 kJ
14 g P, 15 g F, 64 g CH

1 Make a yeast dough from the flour, yeast, 100 ml lukewarm water, a pinch of salt and 4 tablespoons of olive oil. Leave to prove for an hour.

2 Skin, deseed and dice the tomatoes. Peel and chop the onions and garlic, and sauté in 1 tablespoon of hot olive oil. Add the tomatoes, season with salt, pepper, sugar and oregano, and boil down a little until it is a smooth tomato sauce.

3 Roll out the dough and place in the oiled pizza pan, forming a crust around the edge. Spread with the tomato sauce. Scatter over 25 g Pecorino. Place the pepper, sliced into strips, on top. Cut the Gorgonzola into fine dice and chop the chilli finely. Place everything on top of the pizza. Scatter over the rest of the Pecorino and drizzle with the herb oil. Bake in the oven at 220 °C (Gas Mark 7, fan oven 200 °C) for approx. 20 minutes.

Potato pizza
with Parmesan

Makes 1 round pizza

250 g flour

25 g fresh yeast

salt

6 tbsp olive oil

400 g tomatoes

2 onions

2 garlic cloves

pepper

½ tsp sugar

½ tsp dried oregano

500 g potatoes

1 tsp freshly chopped rosemary

75 g grated Parmesan

Preparation time: 35 minutes
(plus resting and baking time)
Per pizza approx. 345 kcal/1444 kJ
18 g P, 33 g F, 68 g CH

1 Make a yeast dough from the flour, yeast, 100 ml of lukewarm water, a pinch of salt and 4 tablespoons of olive oil. Leave to prove for an hour. Skin, deseed and dice the tomatoes. Peel and chop the onions and garlic, and sauté in 1 tablespoon of hot olive oil. Add the tomatoes, season with salt, pepper, sugar and oregano, and boil down until it is a smooth tomato sauce.

2 Roll out the dough and place in an oiled pizza pan. Pull the dough to form a crust and leave to prove. Spread with the tomato sauce. Peel the potatoes, cut into fine slices and place on the pizza. Sprinkle over salt, pepper, rosemary and Parmesan. Drizzle over the rest of the olive oil. Bake in the oven at 200 °C (Gas Mark 6, fan oven 180 °C) for approx. 35 minutes.

Amaretto parfait
with figs

Serves 4

3 eggs
125 g sugar
3 tbsp amaretto
300 ml whipped cream
seeds of ½ vanilla pod
4 figs
2 tbsp Cognac

Preparation time: 20 minutes
Per serving approx. 425 kcal/
1779 kJ
8 g P, 28 g F, 29 g CH

1 Separate one of the eggs. In a warm bain-marie, stir 2 eggs and the egg yolk from the separated egg with 90 g sugar until frothy. Slowly pour in the amaretto and stir the mixture for another 5 minutes.

2 Add the cream to the vanilla seeds and mix together with the egg froth. Pour into 4 pudding moulds and freeze for approx. 3 hours. Cut the figs into quarters and marinate with the Cognac and 35 g sugar in a bowl. Turn the parfait out onto dessert plates and serve with the marinated figs. A fruit sauce would make a good accompaniment.

Torta al limone
Italian lemon cake

Serves 4

12 large eggs

175 g sugar

1 sachet vanilla sugar

150 g chopped almonds

zest and juice of 4 untreated
   lemons

zest of 1 untreated orange

300 g wheat flour

½ tsp salt

butter for greasing

icing sugar

Preparation time: 20 minutes
(plus baking time)
Per serving approx. 465 kcal/
1947 kJ
19 g P, 21 g F, 50 g CH

1 Separate the eggs. Beat the egg yolks in a bowl until very frothy. Gradually add the sugar, vanilla sugar, almonds, lemon zest, lemon juice, orange zest and stir until creamy. Add the flour and salt to the mixture and stir thoroughly. Beat the egg whites until stiff and fold into the cake mixture with a fork until it forms a smooth batter.

2 Pour the batter into a greased loaf pan (25 cm) and bake for an hour in the oven at 170 °C (Gas Mark 3, fan oven 150 °C). Turn the cake out onto a wire rack and sprinkle with icing sugar.

Ricotta ice cream
with espresso

Serves 4

125 ml espresso coffee

500 g ricotta

100 g sugar

4 egg yolks

3 tbsp cream

1 tsp vanilla sugar

4 tbsp Marsala

2 tbsp cocoa powder

Preparation time: 15 minutes
(plus freezing time)
Per serving approx. 428 kcal/
1792 kJ
20 g P, 28 g F, 33 g CH

1 Leave the espresso to cool. Strain the ricotta through a sieve and mix with the espresso. Stir the sugar and egg yolks together until frothy. Beat the cream until stiff, then stir in the vanilla sugar and Marsala. Mix the espresso and ricotta mixture and the egg froth together, then fold in the cream. Pour the mixture into a bowl or rectangular dish and cover with cling film. Freeze for approx. 3 hours until set.

2 You can put the ricotta ice cream into small bowls using an ice cream scoop, cut into slices or spoon onto waffles. Serve sprinkled with cocoa powder.

Cannoli

with ricotta filling

Serves 4

25 g butter
125 g sugar
2 eggs
2½ tbsp milk
3 tbsp vanilla sugar
pinch of salt
150 g wheat flour
oil for deep frying
500 g ricotta
2 tbsp orange liqueur
100 g mixed chopped
    candied orange and
    lemon peel
50 g candied cherries
90 g chopped dark chocolate
icing sugar

Preparation time: 30 minutes
(plus cooling time)
Per serving approx. 863 kcal/
3613 kJ
25 g P, 39 g F, 101 g CH

1 Mix the butter with 25 g sugar, 1 egg, 2½ table-spoons of milk, 2 tablespoons of vanilla sugar, salt and flour until it forms a smooth dough. Cover and stand in a cool place for 2 hours.

2 Roll the dough out until it is 2 mm thick, then cut into 16 squares (12 x 12 cm). Place bamboo or metal rods (15 cm long, 2 cm diameter) diagonally across the pieces of dough, wrap the opposite corners around the rods and brush with the whisked egg. Deep fry the cannoli in the hot oil until golden brown, then remove the rods and leave the rolls of pastry to dry and cool.

3 Mix the ricotta with the orange liqueur, candied fruits, the rest of the sugar, the vanilla sugar and the chocolate. Fill the cannoli with the mixture and sprinkle with icing sugar.

Crespelle
with strawberries

Serves 4

3 eggs
250 ml milk
5 tbsp mineral water
100 g flour
80 g sugar
1 pinch of salt
5 tbsp clarified butter
2 tbsp butter
120 ml white wine
120 ml orange liqueur
300 g strawberries
zest of ½ untreated lemon

Preparation time: 20 minutes
Per serving approx.
1147 kcal/4802 kJ
11 g P, 91 g F, 55 g CH

1. Mix the eggs with the milk and 5 tablespoons of mineral water in a bowl. Stir in the flour, gradually add 30 g sugar and then the pinch of salt. Mix everything until it forms a smooth batter and leave to rest for 10 minutes. Heat the clarified butter in a pan and fry the batter in batches to make thin pancakes. Keep warm.

2. Heat the butter in a pan and caramelise the rest of the sugar.

3. Gradually add the white wine and orange liqueur and bring to a boil, stirring, until it forms a syrup. Cut the strawberries into small pieces. Add to the pan and heat through. Spoon onto the pancakes while still warm, scatter over the zest and fold the pancakes.

Lemon semifreddo
with rum

Serves 4

250 ml mandarin juice

250 ml orange juice

250 ml grapefruit juice

125 ml lime juice

200 g sugar

100 ml rum

orange zest

Preparation time: 20 minutes
(plus freezing time)
Per serving approx. 377 kcal/
1578 kJ
1 g P, 1 g F, 72 g CH

1 Pour the freshly pressed juices through a strainer and mix with 250 ml water. Add the sugar and rum and mix everything together well. Pour into a metal bowl and leave to set for several hours in the freezer.

2 Stir with a fork or whisk several times while freezing. Serve garnished with orange zest.

Panna cotta
Italian cream pudding

Serves 4

1 vanilla pod
400 ml cream
40 g sugar
3 gelatine leaves

Preparation time: 20 minutes
(plus cooling time)
Per serving approx. 330 kcal/
1380 kJ
4 g P, 30 g F, 13 g CH

1 Slice the vanilla pod lengthways and scrape out the seeds with a sharp knife. Heat the cream with the vanilla seeds, vanilla pod and sugar in a bowl inside a bain-marie and simmer for at least 10 minutes. Soak the gelatine in cold water.

2 Remove the pot from the heat and take out the vanilla pod. Squeeze out the gelatine leaves and stir them into the cream. Return the pot to the heat and dissolve the gelatine while stirring the mixture over a low heat.

3 Rinse out 4 dessert bowls with cold water, fill with the cooked cream and leave to set in the fridge for 4–5 hours. Turn onto dessert plates before serving and garnish to taste.

Tiramisu
the classic Italian dessert

Serves 4

2 egg yolks

2 tbsp sugar

350 g Mascarpone

2 tbsp Amaretto

100 g sponge fingers

50 ml cold espresso coffee

2–3 tbsp unsweetened cocoa powder

Preparation time: 20 minutes (plus cooling time)

Per serving approx. 520 kcal/ 2170 kJ

7 g P, 42 g F, 28 g CH

1 Put the egg yolks and sugar in a bowl and use an electric whisk to beat the mixture until it is frothy. Add the Mascarpone spoonful by spoonful and add Amaretto to taste, stirring constantly.

2 Cover the bottom of a flat baking dish or serving bowl with half of the sponge fingers. Drizzle some espresso over the top, followed by a layer of half of the Mascarpone cream. Follow this with another layer of sponge fingers, more espresso and the other half of the Mascarpone cream.

3 Cover the tiramisu and leave in the fridge for at least 4 hours so that the flavours can develop well. Sprinkle cocoa powder over the dessert before serving.

Crêpes Suzette
French orange pancakes

Serves 4

2 eggs

200 ml milk

salt

80 g wheat flour

220 g sugar

100 g butter

6 untreated oranges

4 tbsp orange liqueur
(e.g. Cointreau)

Preparation time: 40 minutes
(plus cooking time)
Per serving approx. 660 kcal/
2760 kJ
9 g P, 26 g F, 90 g CH

1 Whisk the eggs with the milk. Add the salt, flour and 2 tablespoons of sugar, and mix everything to a smooth batter. Froth up half of the butter in a pan, and when it is golden brown, stir into the batter.

2 To make the sauce, wash 3 oranges in hot water and remove the peel in fine strips. Squeeze these 3 oranges and mix the juice with the orange peel and the rest of the sugar in a pot. Bring to a boil and reduce down to a runny syrup over a high heat.

3 Peel the remaining oranges, completely removing the white skin. Cut the segments from their membranes. Collect any juice and add to the syrup.

4 Froth up some butter in 2 coated pans. Pour a ladleful of batter into each, cook the crêpes on both sides until golden brown and then place on a wire rack. Cover with a tea towel and keep warm. Make 12 golden brown crêpes in this way.

5 When all of the crêpes are done, divide the orange segments between them. Fold the crêpes up and place next to each other in 1 or 2 pans. Spoon the sugar syrup and orange liqueur over the top. Warm everything through once again and flambé by setting fire to the liqueur with a long match. Serve immediately.

Mousse au chocolat
French chocolate cream

Serves 4

100 g dark chocolate

2 eggs

1 tbsp sugar

250 ml cream

4 decorative chocolate
hearts

fresh fruit for decoration

icing sugar

Preparation time: 20 minutes
(plus cooking and cooling time)
Per serving approx. 390 kcal/
1630 kJ
7 g P, 33 g F, 17 g CH

1 Chop the chocolate finely with a large kitchen knife. Melt the chocolate pieces in a bowl in a bain-marie, stirring often. As soon as the chocolate has melted, take the pot off the heat and leave to cool a little.

2 Separate the eggs. Pour the egg whites into a bowl and use an electric whisk to beat them until they form stiff peaks.

3 Mix the egg yolks with the sugar in another bowl until frothy, then carefully stir in the warm, melted chocolate.

4 Beat the cream with an electric whisk until stiff. When the chocolate has cooled a little, fold in 1 tablespoon of the egg whites. Continue to fold in the egg whites and cream in spoonfuls. Do not stir too vigorously, as otherwise the egg whites and cream will collapse.

5 Pour the mousse into cold, rinsed dessert bowls and leave to cool in the fridge for 3–4 hours until they are firm. Place the decorative chocolate hearts and fresh fruit on top before serving, and dust with icing sugar.

Sicilian
watermelon dessert

Serves 4

1 watermelon
50 g cornflour
120 g sugar
½ tsp ground cinnamon
1 pinch of ground cloves
30 chocolate drops

Preparation time: approx.
15 minutes (plus chilling time)
Per serving approx. 213 kcal/
889 kJ
0 g P, 2 g F, 48 g CH

1 Peel the watermelon, cut into small pieces, remove the seeds and purée the flesh in a blender. Measure out 800 ml.

2 Mix the cornflour with a little melon purée and put in a pan with the remaining purée and other ingredients (except the chocolate drops). Bring to the boil and simmer for 2–3 minutes whilst stirring constantly.

3 Put the mixture into a large pudding dish or small moulds and allow to stand in the refrigerator for a few hours until firm. Turn out onto dessert plates and serve decorated with chocolate drops.

Crème brûlée
with fruit

Serves 4

125 ml milk
125 ml cream
2 eggs
2 egg yolks
65 g icing sugar
seeds from ½ vanilla pod
6 tbsp sugar for browning
fresh seasonal fruit

Preparation time: 15 minutes
(plus baking and cooling time)
Per serving approx. 292 kcal/
1226 kJ
7 g P, 17 g F, 26 g CH

1 Pre-heat the oven to 150 °C (Gas Mark 2, fan oven 125 °C). Mix the milk with the cream, eggs, egg yolks, icing sugar and vanilla seeds.

2 Pour the egg mixture into four small, flat, oven-proof dishes and place in a large baking tin filled with water. Bake in the oven for 35 minutes, until the mixture has set.

3 Take the dishes out of the oven, leave to cool and leave in the fridge overnight. Sprinkle the *crème* with sugar shortly before serving and place under a hot grill until the sugar begins to brown. Fresh fruit makes a good accompaniment.

Stuffed peaches
with amaretti

Serves 4

4 large, ripe peaches

juice of ½ lemon

65 g amaretti

30 ml Marsala

25 g butter

½ tsp ground vanilla

30 g icing sugar

1 egg yolk

Preparation time: approx.
15 minutes (plus soaking and
baking time)
Per serving approx. 235 kcal/
989 kJ
3 g P, 10 g F, 31 g CH

1 Pre-heat the oven to 180 °C (Gas Mark 4, fan oven 160 °C). Wash the peaches and pat them dry. Halve the fruits and remove the stones. Enlarge the hollow where the stone was using a spoon and drizzle the peaches with lemon juice.

2 Crush the amaretti with a rolling pin. Soak them with the Marsala in a bowl and allow to stand for 10 minutes. Beat the soft butter until foamy and mix with the amaretti mixture, vanilla powder, icing sugar and egg yolk.

3 Place the peach halves in an ovenproof dish. Fill with the amaretti mixture and bake in the oven for about 35 minutes.

Ice cream soufflé
with orange liqueur

Serves 4–6

150 ml cream

250 g sugar

6 eggs

50 g ground almonds

100 ml orange liqueur

greaseproof paper

4 tsp chopped almonds

Preparation time: 30 minutes
(plus cooking and freezing time)
Per serving approx. 433 kcal/
1818 kJ
9 g P, 18 g F, 47 g CH

1 Beat the cream until stiff. Place the sugar in a pot with 250 ml water and boil down, stirring, until it forms a syrup.

2 Separate the eggs. Beat the egg whites until they form stiff peaks and slowly stir in the sugar syrup.

3 Beat the egg yolks in a pot with a little water until they are frothy – they should not clot. Fold the sugar and egg whites into the egg yolk mixture.

4 Toast the ground almonds in a dry pan. Stir the almonds and orange liqueur into the egg mixture. Leave to cool and mix with the cream.

5 Line a soufflé dish with greaseproof paper, allowing more room towards the top. Pour the mixture over the edge and leave to freeze for at least 6 hours. Remove the paper before serving and garnish with chopped almonds.

Index